Contents

GU00497160

Introduction

The rewards of making your own soft furnishings are both practical and personal. You can save money by making items at home which would cost a great deal more to buy in a store; it is also much easier to get exactly the result you want, in exactly the colour you want, if you choose the materials and make your furnishings at home.

Whether you start in a modest way by making a cushion or whether you make your own curtains, the satisfaction of having chosen and made them to suit your home will amply repay the time and money spent.

It would be foolish to start on a project without the necessary tools, and a few basic tools are important when making your own soft furnishings. If you are lucky enough to have somewhere to work, a spare bedroom perhaps, where the equipment can be left out undisturbed until the project is finished, you are fortunate indeed. Otherwise working space must be improvised. An uncluttered table is needed to cut fabric for cushions and lampshades, a large area of clean floor is better for curtains. A steam iron, or a dry iron and a wet cloth, on an ironing board at your side while you work, will ensure that all seams are pressed as work progresses.

Before embarking on a project read the instructions through and make a check list of all the materials and tools you will need; nothing is more maddening than to find you have no suitable sewing cotton on a Saturday night.

Tools for Soft Furnishings

(The tools required for upholstery are different and are listed on page 42.)
Scissors A large pair of cutting-out scissors about 20cm (8in) long; these must be kept for cutting fabric only and should not be used for cutting paper or they will become blunt. You will also need a smaller pair of scissors with sharp points for cutting notches in turnings and snipping off ends of thread. *Tape-measure and tailor's chalk* are needed for most jobs; when making curtains it is very useful to have a *metre stick* or *yardstick*—a long wooden rule which makes the measurement of long drops much more accurate than a tape measure. *Pins* must be sharp and not rusted. As a tin or box of pins tends to get spilt it is worth making a wrist pin-cushion; this is a small, sawdust-filled pad stitched to a loop of elastic that threads on the wrist, making the pins easy to reach at all times. A *sewing machine* is a must if you are going to make things for the home, but it doesn't need to be a very versatile one; a zig-zag stitch is an advantage for oversewing raw edges, and generally a heavyweight machine is much more stable when used with long lengths of heavy fabric than a lightweight portable. A *piping foot* can be bought quite cheaply to fit your machine if you don't already have one, and is essential for piped cushions and covers.

Apart from these items, just normal sewing equipment is required: needles, sewing thread, and a thimble if you wear one.

Some of the stitches and seams mentioned in the book with their uses are illustrated in the diagrams opposite.

There are step-by-step instructions or making both simple and complex soft furnishings, starting with cushions and progressing to lampshades, tablecloths, bed-linen, loose covers, upholstery, curtains and making furniture with foam.

I hope you will find this a useful book and that it may inspire you to make some or even all of the things listed. Happy sewing!

Note All the measurements in the book are given in metric followed by the imperial equivalent; as the conversions are sometimes approximate, one system should be used consistently.

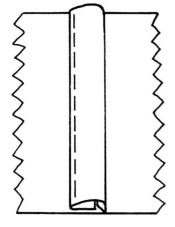

1 Self-bound seam

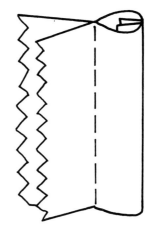

4 French seam

2 Gathering stitch

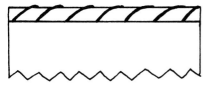

5 Ladder stitch

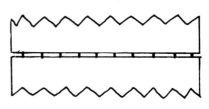

3 Oversewing stitch

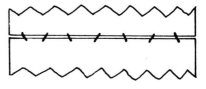

6 Slip stitch

Cushions

On the following pages I will be showing how to make cushion covers for square, round, box and bolster shaped cushions; then how to trim them with piping, pleats, frills and other finishes.

I will also show how to make 'cushion pads' or the cushions themselves and explain the different cushion fillings available and their merits, because if you really want to save money you should make not only the cushion cover but the cushion itself as well. It is really never worth your time and effort making a cushion cover which is then stuffed with filling and therefore cannot be removed for washing or dry-cleaning; you'll find that a cushion pad the exact size and shape you require is quite easy and inexpensive to make.

Cushion Fillings

Feathers

Feathers are the most luxurious and most comfortable filling for soft cushions and scatter cushions. It is quite possible to make your own feather-filled cushions if you are lucky enough to pick up an old feather pillow at a jumble sale or second-hand shop. Make the casing from a feather-proof cambric and make double rows of stitching to prevent the feathers from seeping through the seams. Hang the open casing on a washing line secured firmly with pegs. Choose a fine day when there is no prevailing wind. Hand fill the casing with feathers (some of the feathers will escape, but outdoors should do little harm). Peg the opening together when the casing is full, but not stuffed too tightly. Slipstitch opening with small close stitches, using double thread.

Polyester Fibre

This is the next best thing to feathers and one of the most expensive fillings to buy new. It is very soft, doesn't separate into hard balls, and has the advantage over feathers that it can be washed as well as dry-cleaned. Suitable for all shapes of soft and scatter cushions.

Foam Chips

This is a very inexpensive filling to buy, and in many street markets huge sacks of foam chips can be bought very cheaply indeed. For this reason it is an obvious choice of filling for large floor-cushions or where lots of cushions are required. Its disadvantages are that it is unsuitable for washing as it tends to disintegrate and the dye runs and also that it tends to show a rather lumpy surface through the cushion cover. One way to overcome the lumpiness at little extra cost is to make a padded casing of calico and medium-thick terylene wadding (wadding on the inside) which softens the outline of the foam chips.
Suitable for scatter cushions and floor-cushions but not sag-bags (see next paragraph).

Polystyrene Granules

These granules or 'beads' are the best filling for sag-bags as they are rigid in themselves but because of their size and shape they can be pushed into different shapes. It is important to keep a small amount of granules back after filling the sag-bag in order to 'top up' after a month or so when the granules have settled.
Only suitable for sag-bags.

Foam

This is the most practical filling for box cushions, shaped squab and armchair cushions. It can be bought in several different qualities varying from light-density to one which is suitable as a mattress. It can be bought ready-cut in a variety of shapes and sizes and can also be supplied cut to the shape of your own pattern or template.

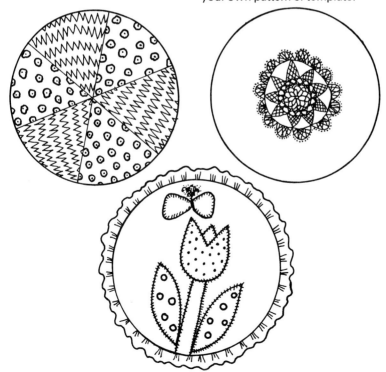

Cushions

Square Cushion

Cushion Cover

You will need two squares of fabric the
measurement you wish the cover to be,
plus 3cm (1¼in). A zip fastener about
3–5cm (1¼–2in) smaller, matching
sewing thread and a zipper-foot for
your machine.

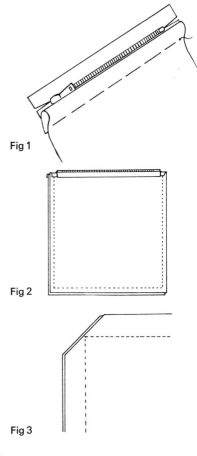

Fig 1

Fig 2

Fig 3

Fold 1.5cm (⅝in) of one of the pieces
of fabric under along one edge and lay
along the centre of the zip, right side up.
Tack fabric to zip (Fig 1). Machine
fabric to zip along tacking line, then
sew second piece of fabric to other side
of zip in the same way. Remove
tacking threads and open zip a little
way.

Fold one of the pieces of fabric over
the other, right sides together with raw
edges aligned. Tack round other three
sides and from ends of zip taking
1.5cm (⅝in) turnings (Fig 2). Machine
along tacking lines and remove
tacking. Clip corners (Fig 3). Turn to
right side and poke out corners with
the point of a pencil, then press.

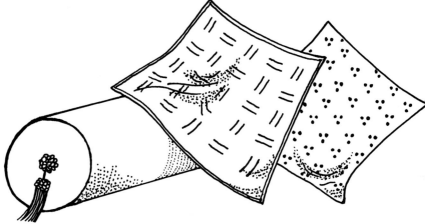

Cushion Pad

Make casing from calico in the same way as cushion cover, but omitting zip. Stuff with chosen filling then slipstich opening. The cushion pad can be the same size as a plain cover but should be about 6mm ($\frac{1}{4}$in) smaller than piped or frilled covers to allow for the extra turnings.

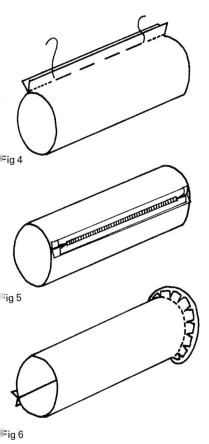

Fig 4

Fig 5

Fig 6

Bolster

Bolster Cover

Decide what size you want your bolster to be, that is, the diameter of the round ends and the length of the body. The piece of fabric for the body section of the bolster cover will be an oblong measuring this length, plus 1.5cm ($\frac{5}{8}$in) for turnings, by the circumference of the end, plus the same allowance for turnings.

To calculate this circumference, cut out the round ends first and measure round 1.5cm ($\frac{5}{8}$in) from the edge with a tape-measure (this is *very roughly* just over three times the diameter).

Fold the oblong body piece down the length of the bolster with right sides together and machine a little way from each end taking 1.5cm ($\frac{5}{8}$in) turnings so that a space is left the length of the zip. Tack this opening together and press seam (see Fig 4). Tack the zip in place, right side up on the wrong side of the tacked opening (see Fig 5). Turn fabric to the right side and machine zip in place, then remove tacking. Turn to wrong side again and open zip a little way. Pin one of the round ends, right sides together, to one end of the body taking 1.5cm ($\frac{5}{8}$in) turnings and clipping turnings of body as in Fig 6. Machine and repeat with other end. Turn to right side through zip and press.

Bolster Pad

Make in the same way but omit zip and slipstitch opening after pad has been stuffed. Pad can be the same size as a plain cover but should be cut about 0.5cm smaller on each edge for a piped or frilled cover to allow for the extra turnings.

7

Cushions

Round Cushion

Decide what size diameter you want your cushion to be, then cut fabric as follows : Take two squares of fabric measuring at least the diameter you want your cushion to be, plus 3cm ($1\frac{1}{4}$in) for turnings. Lay both squares on top of each other so that the edges are exactly aligned. Fold the double fabric over in half, then fold in half again in the opposite direction like a handkerchief. From the corner which is the centre of the fabric fold over diagonally (see Fig 1). Place end of tape-measure at central point and measure radius (half the diameter) plus turning all across fabric as in Fig 1. Cut along marked line through all thicknesses of fabric. Open out circles. Pin right side of zip (about one-third length of circumference) to right side of one of the rounds taking 1.5cm ($\frac{5}{8}$in) turnings. Machine, and repeat with other edge of zip and other round (match fabric pattern at this point). Cut notches in turnings as in Fig 2. Open zip a little way, then pin together the edges of the remainder of the circle and machine, taking the same turning. Cut notches as before and press.

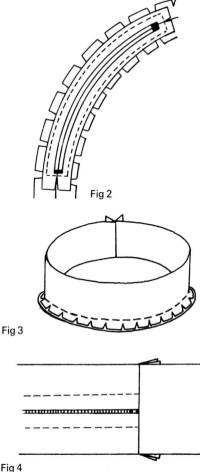

Fig 2

Fig 3

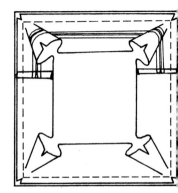

Fig 4

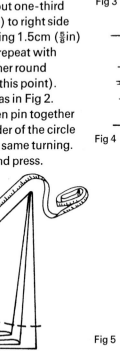

Fig 1

Fig 5

8

Round Cushion Pad

Make in exactly the same way but omit zip and slipstitch opening after stuffing.

Round Cushion with Gusset

You will need two circles of fabric the size of the foam plus turnings. To cut these, lay foam on double fabric, wrong side up. Draw around with tailor's chalk then cut out allowing for turnings (all turnings should be 1.5cm ($\frac{5}{8}$in)).

For gusset : a strip of fabric the circumference of the foam plus turnings, by the depth of the foam plus turnings. If it is not possible to cut this strip in one piece, make one join exactly halfway round.

It is not very practical to have a zip in gussetted round cushions as the zip has to run nearly halfway round the cushion to allow the foam to be inserted, and as the cushion has no definite 'back' the zip tends to show. It is easier to slipstitch part of the seam together after the foam has been inserted, unpicking stitches to remove the cover for cleaning.

Tack and machine the short ends of the gusset strip, right sides together. Press turning open. Tack and machine gusset to top of cover, right sides together. Clip turnings of gusset (Fig 3), then repeat with bottom of cover, leaving a little under half of the seam open. Clip turnings and turn to right side. Insert foam and slipstitch seam opening.

Box Cushion Cover

For the top and bottom of the cover you will need : two squares (or rectangles) of fabric the size of the top of your foam block, plus turnings. All turnings should be 1.5cm ($\frac{5}{8}$in). A strong zip fastener 12–16cm (5–7in) longer than one side measurement of block (if you have a rectangle of foam, the measurement of a long side).

For the gusset: one strip of fabric the length of the zip plus turnings, by the depth of the foam block plus turnings and plus an extra 3cm ($1\frac{1}{4}$in) to allow for the insertion of the zip ; a second strip the remaining length of the border plus turnings, by the depth of the foam plus turnings. If you do not have enough fabric to cut this second gusset strip in one piece, make joins at the corners of the cushion.

Cut the zip-length strip of fabric in half lengthways and insert zip as described for square cushion cover, page 6, making 1.5cm ($\frac{5}{8}$in) overlap each edge of zip. Lay gusset strip with zip on second gusset strip, right sides together and short ends meeting. Tack and machine these short sides together so that the slider and the stop-end of the zip are just free of the seam, and press the turnings away from the zip (see Fig 4).

Tack and machine the complete border to the top of the cushion, centring the zip on the side that will be the back of the finished cushion. Clip the gusset turnings at the corners, and make corresponding nicks in the turning of the gusset directly above the corner as a guide for sewing the corners of the bottom piece of the cover (see Fig 5). Open the zip a little way and tack and machine the gusset to the bottom of the cover, matching the notches to the corners. Open zip completely, turn cover to right side and press. Gently but firmly insert foam block and do up zip.

Cushions

Decorative Edges

All the cushions described can be trimmed by adding piping, frills, pleats, points or fringe around the edge seams.

Piping

This looks particularly good on box or gussetted cushions; it can be made to match or contrast the body of the cushion cover, and consists of a cord covered by a strip of fabric which is inserted into the seam of the cushion cover.

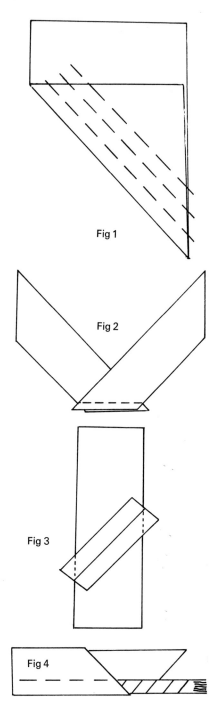

Fig 1

Fig 2

Fig 3

Fig 4

Piping cord comes in several different thicknesses but generally numbers 3 and 4 are most suitable for cushions and loose covers. The fabric covering strips for these sizes should be 4cm (1½in) wide and *must* be cut on the bias, that is, diagonally to the weave of the fabric, otherwise there will not be enough stretch in the piping to go smoothly around the curves without wrinkling.

To cut bias strips
If you do not need a very long strip of bias you can use scraps or cut strips from an oblong as follows : Fold over a corner of the fabric to find the true bias and cut strips as in Fig 1. Machine strips right sides together taking 1.5cm (⅝in) turning as in Fig 2. Use a small machine stitch so that the cord will not show between the stitches. Press seams open, and cut off protruding corners as in Fig 3.

Inserting piping in seam
The bias strip is then folded in half lengthwise, with wrong sides together

10

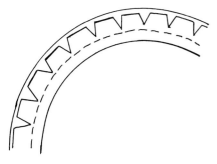

Fig 5

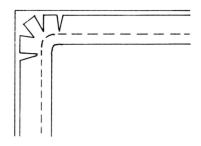

To join piping
When piping cushions, it is necessary to make a join where the ends of the piping meet. Tack the piping around the cushion, stopping a little short of the place where the ends meet. Pull back the fabric covering and cut the cords so they overlap each other 2.5cm (1in). Unravel the cords and cut away 2.5cm (1in) of *two* strands on cord A, and *one* strand on cord B as in Fig 6. Twist the remaining ends and stitch together with sewing thread as in Fig 7. Pull fabric casing together and pin ends so that they fit cord. Machine and press crossway join as in Fig 8.

Fig 6

and placed around the piping cord (Fig 4). The piping is then placed on the right side of the cushion cover front, raw edges meeting around the edge, and then tacked and machined in place. The bottom of the cushion cover (or the gusset strip if the cushion is gussetted) is placed on top, with right sides together, and tacked and then machined close to the cord.

When the edge is curved, as in a round cushion, and at the corners of square cushions, the turnings of the piping must be clipped as in Fig 5.

Fig 7

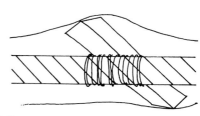

Fig 8

11

Cushions

Decorative Edges

Frilled Edge

Cut a strip of fabric (joined where necessary) $1\frac{1}{2}$ times the outside measurement of your cushion cover. Make the strip twice the width you wish the frill to be, plus turnings.

Machine the short ends of the strip, right sides together and press. Fold the joined strip over lengthways, wrong sides together, and run a gathering thread along the double raw edges, just inside the turning.

Tack the gathered strip around the edge of the right side of the cushion front, raw edges meeting, as in Fig 1, adjusting gathers evenly. Machine frill in place.

Place cushion back on cushion front, right sides together and raw edges meeting. Tack and machine as close to first line of machining as possible. Where frill goes around corner adjust frills as in Fig 2.

Pleated Edge

Cut fabric strip as for frilled edge but allow *three* times the outside measurement of the cushion cover, plus turnings.

Join short ends of strip as for frill. Fold strip lengthwise, wrong sides together and fold pleats as in Fig 4. The pleats should be about 3cm ($1\frac{1}{4}$in) wide but you can make them any size you like, as long as they are all the same size.

Tack pleats together and then tack and machine to cushion front, as for frill. Adjust pleats to fit corners as in Fig 3.

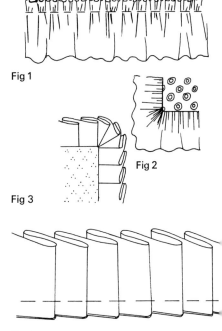

Fig 1

Fig 2

Fig 3

Fig 4

Pointed Edge

Cut squares of fabric 7.5cm (3in), the fabric can contrast or match the cushion cover as you wish. Fold the squares in half, then in half again. Tack the folded squares to the edge of the cushion front and machine in place as in Fig 5.

If the squares do not fit exactly along an edge, overlap them slightly until they fit. Machine cushion cover front to back in the normal way.

Fringed Edge

Buy sufficient fringing to go around the edge of your cushion plus 2cm ($\frac{3}{4}$in). Place fringe on edge of cushion front as in Fig 6 and machine in place. Double back 1cm of fringe edges where they meet.

Fig 5

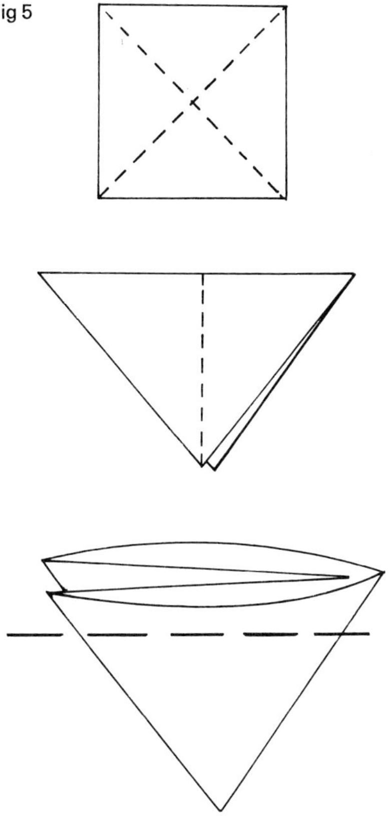

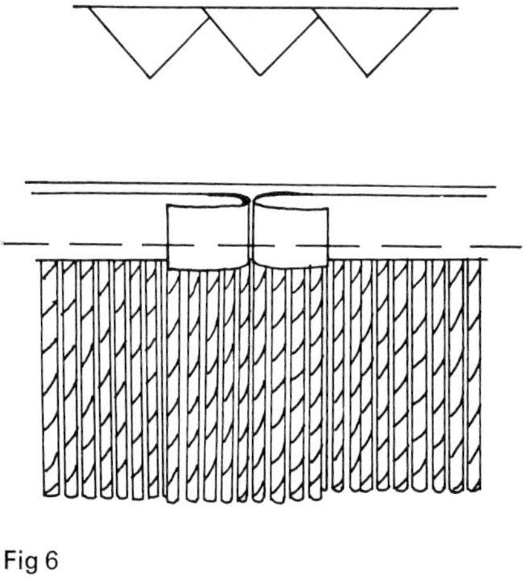

Sag-bag Cushion

This is a large floor cushion loosely filled with a firm filling such as polystyrene granules, as it is loosely filled and 'saggy' it can be pushed and pummelled to form whatever shape you choose and in this way serves as an armchair of infinite variations.

The material for the outer cover must be strong and hard-wearing, canvas, corduroy and vinyl are all suitable. Make an inner cover to contain the granules from calico and an outer cover which can be unstitched or unzipped for cleaning ; make both covers in exactly the same way following the instructions given here.

You will need two circles of 100cm (39in), and a strip 350 × 75cm (11ft 6in × 2ft 6in) ; as suitable fabrics come in many different widths it is better to work out the total amount needed yourself. The circles are best cut without a join but the long strip can be joined as necessary.

With right sides together, pin the long strip to the circle, taking 1cm ($\frac{3}{8}$in) turnings and pleating the strip evenly to fit the circle. Machine (with a small stitch for the inner cover to prevent the granules seeping out) taking 1cm ($\frac{3}{8}$in) turnings. Repeat with other circle and the other edge of the strip, leaving the seam in the strip open for filling with polystyrene granules or to be slipstitched up over inner cover.

Use a bowl or a saucepan to fill the inner cover with granules, then stitch up the opening. A sag-bag this size will need a 0.34cu m (12cu ft) bag of polystyrene granules, these tend to settle after some use and then the sag-bag should be topped up with a smaller quantity.

Fig 6

13

Cushions

Floor Cushions

These are really only giant square cushions, measuring about 1 m (39in) square. As they are so large and have to take a lot of heavy wear a really strong outer cover is most important. Carpet is the traditional covering and a material of this type, such as velour, Dralon or heavy cotton is the most suitable.

Make in the same way as a square cushion (see page 6) making an inner cover of calico to contain the filling and an outer cover with a zip that can be removed for cleaning. A corded piping inserted in the seam looks most effective and adds to the eastern flavour; piping of this sort can be bought at most good haberdashery departments.

Because of the size of the floor cushion the only practical filling is foam chips. Giant sacks of these can be bought very cheaply at many street markets and it is well worth shopping around to find a bargain. A floor cushion 1 m (39in) square will take roughly 0.23cu m (8cu ft) of foam chippings.

Smocked Cushion

These cushions look most effective in a fabric which reflects the light, such as velvet or satin. The cushion has a square area of smocking in the centre which draws the fabric in with a basketweave effect, but by continuing the grid of dots in either direction, keeping the numbering of the dots in sequence, you can adapt these smocking instructions to make whatever size or shape you want.

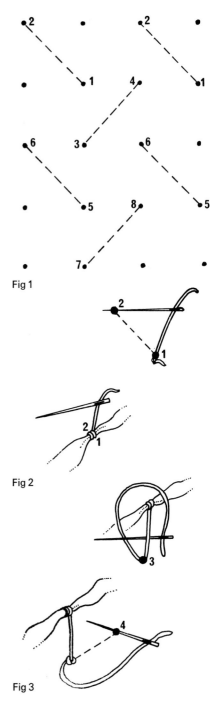

Fig 1

Fig 2

Fig 3

You will need two squares of fabric a little larger than you want the finished cushion to be ; tailors' carbon paper and pencil ; a needle and matching thread.

Using the carbon paper, mark out on the wrong side of one of your pieces of fabric, a square grid of dots, 2cm ($\frac{3}{4}$in) apart both from left to right and up and down. Make the area of dots roughly twice the size you wish the smocked area to be, and centre it in the square of fabric.

The sequence in which the dots should be gathered up is shown in Fig 1. This is done as follows (Fig 2) : working on the wrong side of the fabric, thread needle with matching thread and pick up small piece of fabric at dot 1. Take needle to dot 2 and pull thread tight so that dots 1 and 2 are gathered together, repeat this stitch a couple of times so that gather will hold firm. Take needle to dot 3 and pick up fabric. Then take the needle under the thread between dots 1/2 and 3 and pass needle over loose thread and pull it tight to form a holding-knot so that the thread between dots 1/2 and 3 does not pull tight, as in Fig 3. Now pick up fabric at dot 4 and gather up to dot 3 as you did for dots 1 and 2.

Continue in this way until all the dots are smocked and a basketweave effect has been formed on the right side of the fabric. Lay smocked fabric over cushion pad, wrong side up, and tack to other side of fabric. Trim off any excess fabric leaving turning of 1.5cm ($\frac{5}{8}$in) all round. Make up as for square cushion, inserting piping if desired.

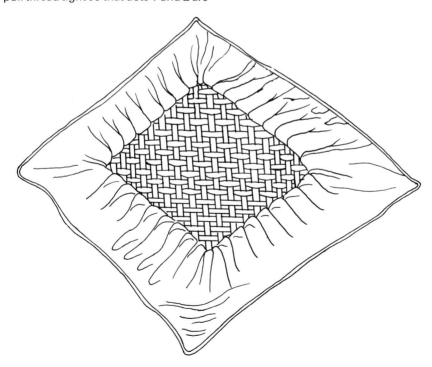

Lampshades

As anyone who has recently bought one will know, lampshades are extremely expensive ; they are also fragile and difficult to transport, so there are many advantages to be gained by making your own. One of these is that you can make shades from fabric that matches your wallpaper or other furnishings, or even save money by making a lampshade from wallpaper left over after decorating, (see page 26) for a really smart co-ordinated look.

Choosing the Frame

There are fashions in lampshades, as in everything else, and it is a good idea before buying a lampshade frame to go to the lighting department of a big store and look at the combinations of bases and shades displayed there.

Having seen the sort of shade you like, work out what size and shape will balance your lamp base. Do this by cutting out a rough outline of the shade in newspaper or brown paper. Hold this up, or better still get a friend to hold it, in front of your lamp and judge whether it is too small, too tall

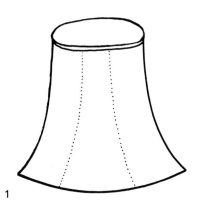

1

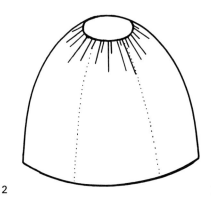

2

3

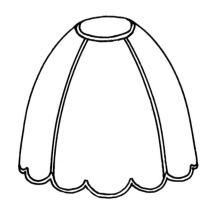

4

or too wide for the lamp base. Keep altering the sheet of paper till you are happy with the result, then buy a lampshade frame as close as possible to these proportions.

Some lampshade frames are very versatile and can be successfully covered by using any one of several different techniques, whereas other frames are really suited to only one method. In the illustrations below some of the most popular styles of frame are shown together with the covering methods that can be used. The various techniques are described on the following pages.

1 Tailored shade with balloon lining
2 Tiffany shade
3 Frilled tiffany shade
4 Tailored tiffany shade
5 Stiffened oval shade
6 Drum shade
7 Coolie shade
8 Pleated paper shade

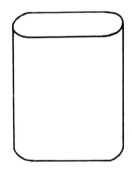

5

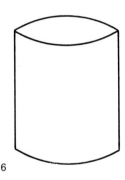

6

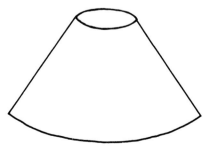

7

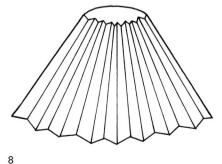

8

Lampshades

Tailored Shade with Balloon Lining (1)

For this and other types it is necessary to bind the frame.

Binding the frame
Use lampshade tape, available from most haberdashery departments, usually about 1.3cm ($\frac{1}{2}$in) wide, a cheap cotton tape bought on a roll or skein. The purpose of the binding is to provide a firm basis on to which the cover and lining will be stitched. Before frames were plastic-covered, the binding also helped to prevent rust, although this is not necessary now. The tape is wound at a diagonal around the struts and knotted to secure the ends of the tape.

To estimate the amount of tape
Measure the length of the struts and the circumference of the top and base of the frame—you will need roughly $2\frac{1}{2}$ times the measurement of each strut and twice the measurement of the circumference.

Bind the upright struts first, winding the tape over the top ring and then binding over the end of the tape, as in Fig 1. The binding must be absolutely firm—pull the end of the tape tight so that it doesn't slip. The binding must also be quite even, so that a smooth surface is obtained, otherwise ugly ridges of binding will appear through the cover.

When you reach the end of a strut, loop the tape through itself and pull it tight to form a finishing knot, Fig 2. When taping the top and bottom rings, start and finish at a strut and wind the tape around each side of the strut in a criss-cross so that there are no gaps in the tape.

To estimate fabric for cover
The fabric is fitted to the frame with the fabric selvedge running upright to the frame. Measure half the circumference of your frame (at the widest point) and the height; you will need two pieces of fabric this size plus 30cm (12in) in each direction for the cover and the lining. If you can cut two pieces this size from one width of fabric you will only need to buy the length, plus 30cm (12in). If your fabric is not wide enough to do this you must buy twice this amount.

If you wish to trim the top and bottom edges of the shade with bias strip (see page 27 for trimmings), you must buy extra fabric to allow for this.

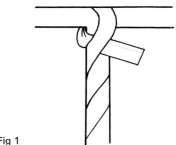

Fig 1

Fig 2

18

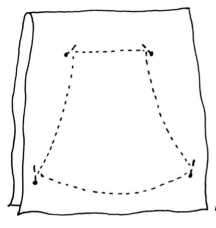

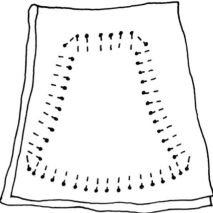

Fig 3

Fig 4

To fit fabric on frame

Fold fabric in half across the width with right sides inside. Place some pins around edges and in corners of fabric to hold the two layers of fabric firmly together. Pin the fabric to half the frame (at points where gimbal meets frame), placing first pins at halfway points on top and bottom edges of frame and stretching fabric evenly between these four pins, see Fig 3.

Starting at the centre of the two side struts and working outwards, stretch and pin the fabric about every 2.5cm (1in), smoothing out the fullness as you pin. Then stretch and pin fabric on top and bottom rings, placing pins as in Fig 4. Adjust and re-pin fabric as necessary until all wrinkles are removed and fabric is quite taut.

Place additional pins between pins on side struts so that fabric is pinned every 12mm ($\frac{3}{4}$in). With a soft pencil, mark side struts and a little of the top

and bottom rings on to the fabric. Remove all the pins except those holding the fabric together around the edge and cut the fabric along the fold. Seam fabric along pencil line with a small machine stitch. Pull the fabric as you sew to give the seams sufficient elasticity to pull over the frame without breaking. Trim seam turnings to 1cm ($\frac{3}{8}$in) and press seams, pressing both turnings in the same direction.

Make up lining in exactly the same way. Turn cover to right side and place over the top of frame, pull down over frame till pencil marks align with top and bottom rings and seams align with, and are neatly behind, side struts. Pin fabric around top and bottom rings, starting at side struts and pulling fabric taut until there are no wrinkles. With double matching thread, oversew fabric to top and bottom rings. Trim fabric close to stiches.

Lampshades

Tailored Shade with Balloon Lining (2)

To apply lining
Press lining as for cover. Place lining inside shade so that seams face towards the cover and are aligned with the side struts. Pull fabric over the top and bottom rings and pin taut without wrinkles. Unpick a little of the side seams so that the lining can be pulled each side of the gimbal, as in Fig 1. Stitch the lining to the outside of the top and bottom rings close to outer cover stitches. In this way the inside of the shade is perfectly neat and all the stitching will be covered by the trimming.

Cut lining fabric away close to stitches.

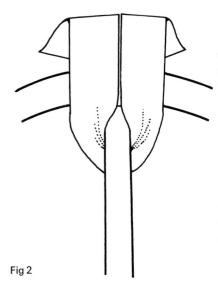

Fig 2

To neaten the lining around the gimbal
Cut a folded crossway strip (see page 27) from lining fabric, and fold this around the gimbal as in Fig 2. Bring the ends of the crossway strip around to the front of the bottom ring and stitch level with lining stitches, then cut off ends of crossway strip close to stitches, as in Fig 3. In this way the ends will be covered by the trimming.

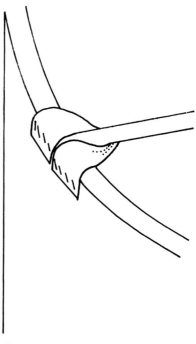

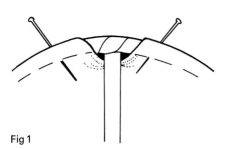

Fig 1

Fig 3

Tiffany Shade

These lampshades are fashionable and very quick and easy to make as they do not have to be lined and as they are not tailored do not require any hand sewing.

To estimate fabric required
Measure the diameter of the frame at its widest point, add to this 3cm (1¼in); measure the frame from the top to the bottom ring, stretching the tape over a strut, and add to this 8cm (3in); you will need a piece of fabric this size and some narrow elastic.

Make a french seam down the side of the piece of fabric. To do this, first fold fabric wrong sides together and make a seam taking 6mm (¼in) turnings. Then turn fabric to wrong side and seam again taking 1cm (⅜in) turning; in this way the raw edges are neatly encased in the seam so a lining is not necessary.

Make a 1cm (⅜in) machined hem top and bottom of the seamed fabric and unpick sufficient of the seam to insert elastic through these hems. Place fabric tube over frame, right side out and pull up both lengths of elastic so that fabric is held firmly in place as in Fig 4.

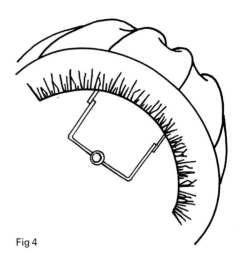

Fig 4

Frilled Tiffany Shade

Make in same way but add a hemmed strip about 6cm (2½in) wide above top hem, and a gathered frill of the same width to come just above bottom ring of frame (measure this distance from top hem). Fit shade in the same way. Alternatively add broderie anglaise in place of the frills.

Lampshades

Tailored Tiffany Shade

A lined and tailored tiffany shade can be made in the same way as the tailored shade (page 18) but because of the shape of the frame a balloon lining is not suitable. The lining is therefore applied in exactly the same way as the cover, stitched on from the front before the cover is applied. A panel of fabric is usually applied to cover three struts on a frame with twelve upright struts.

A tiffany frame with a scalloped base must be covered by the tailored method shown in Figs 1-4; the joins between the panels look neatest if covered with crossway strip.
The lining, top and base, is trimmed, turned to the front, stuck and covered with crossway strip.

Unlined Tailored Tiffany Shade

This is much simpler to make than the lined tailored tiffany shade and can be made without any hand sewing.

To estimate fabric required
Measure frame from top to bottom ring, stretching tape over strut; add to this measurement 4cm ($\frac{5}{8}$in) for hem at bottom edge and bound top edge, plus another 5cm (2in) to gather under frame, making 10cm (4in) allowance in all.

Measure half the circumference of the base of the frame, then add to this 4cm ($1\frac{1}{2}$in) for turnings. Cut two pieces of fabric slightly larger than this measurement (to allow for stretching) on the *bias* of the fabric. Cut also a bias strip 3cm ($1\frac{3}{4}$in) wide, the

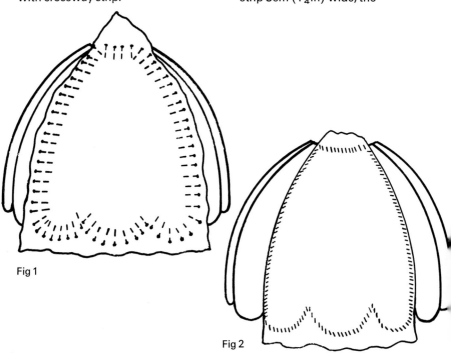

Fig 1

Fig 2

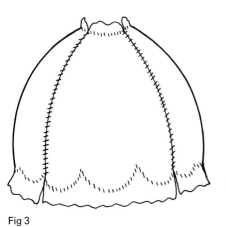

Fig 3

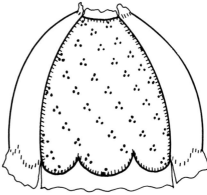

Fig 4

circumference of the top ring, plus 3cm (1¼in).

Pin the two pieces of fabric around the frame *right* side out, in the same way as for a tailored shade, making the joins align with the two side struts. When the fabric is completely taut and smooth in all directions, remove top and bottom pins but leave side-seam pins in place. Slip fabric off frame towards the top. Trim off excess fabric at side seams to within 1.5cm (⅝in) of the pins.

Make french seams down sides as follows : machine 6mm (¼in) from cut edge, then remove pins and turn fabric to wrong side. Make a second line of machining 1cm (⅜in) from the edge ; in this way the raw edges are neatly encased in the seams and a lining is not necessary. Replace fabric over frame, aligning seams with struts, and mark with tailors' chalk 2cm (¾in) from top ring and 7cm (2¾in) from bottom ring. Remove fabric and cut along chalk line. Make a machined hem at the bottom of

the fabric, 1cm (⅜in) wide, with a small gap through which to insert elastic.

To bind top edge
Machine short edges of bias strip, right sides together, and press seam open. Pin strip to top edge of fabric, aligning seam to a side seam, and with right side of strip to wrong side of fabric, raw edges matching. Machine, taking 1cm (⅜in) turning. Turn strip over to right side of fabric and tuck in 1cm (⅜in). Pin in place and machine close to folded edge so that only this second row of machining shows.

Make a small nick in the side seam of the bias strip and thread narrow elastic through bound edge. Thread narrow elastic through bottom hem. Place shade over frame and align seams with struts. Draw up elastic top and bottom and stitch ends of elastic together. Cut off ends of elastic close to stitching and push ends of elastic into seam. Slipstitch up gaps in seam.

Lampshades

Stiffened Fabric Lampshades

Most shops selling lampshade-making
equipment now sell a variety of ready
stiffened fabric. This has a stiff but
flexible card or plastic back. It comes in
a few patterns and a good selection of
plain colours. The textures of the fabric
range from fine silk-type surfaces to
chunky openwork hessians. Drum-
shaped shades, coolie-shaped shades
and straight-sided oval shades are all
suitable for this type of covering. See
Figs 5-7, page 17.

The advantages of making a drum
shade from stiffened fabrics are that
quite a large frame can be made easily
and much more cheaply than a bought
shade. The drum shades can be made
on two lampshade rings, unconnected
by any side struts, which means that
when the lamp is lit there are no struts
to impede the light. The rings must be
the same size and one must carry a light
fitting. Decide the height and the
diameter you want your shade to be,
see page 16, and buy the correct size
rings accordingly.

To estimate fabric for drum shade
You will need stiffened fabric the height
you wish your shade to be, by the
diameter of the rings, plus 2cm ($\frac{3}{4}$in)
for side overlap. You will also need
some spring clothes-pegs, clear
adhesive and braid to decorate top and
bottom rings.

Bind the frame as for tailored shade,
page 18. Using clothes-pegs, clip the
fabric to the rings, so that the edge of
the fabric comes just level with the
covered rings and does not stick up

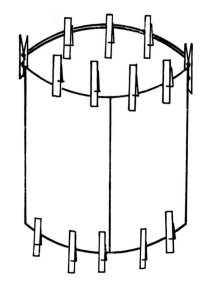

Fig 1

above or below them. Hold the overlap
in place with a clothes-peg. See Fig 1.

Using double thread and a short,
strong needle oversew through the
stiffened fabric to the bound frame
from the front, see Fig 2. These
stitches will be covered by the braid.
Start the stitching about 2cm ($\frac{3}{4}$in)
from the overlap and finish the
stitching the same distance away.
Trim the overlap down to 1cm ($\frac{3}{8}$in) by
cutting down a lightly ruled line and
continue blanket stitch over overlap.

Using an old knife, very carefully
spread clear adhesive on to join,
making sure no adhesive gets on front
of frame. Press join closed with fingers
until the overlap is stuck. This join will
be very neat and will not require
covering with braid. To trim shade, see
section on trimming, page 27.

Straight-sided Oval Shade

This is made exactly like the drum shade but the frame for an oval shade will have side struts which should be bound. Make the join in the fabric on one of the curved sides of the oval shade.

Coolie-shaped Shade

This is made in the same way as the drum and the oval but as the top circumference of this shade is smaller than the base, the fabric has to be cut in a curve. This is made using stiffened fabric.

To estimate fabric required

If the shade is to be quite small you may be able to cut the fabric in one piece and have only one side join ; but it is more likely that it will have to be made in two pieces with joins.

Make a brown paper pattern by laying the frame on its side on the paper and gently rolling it halfway round, marking the top and bottom edges of the frame on the paper as you roll. Cut out the paper along the marked lines and try the pattern against the frame to check that it is accurate. Make a second pattern for the other half of the shade. The two pieces of fabric can be cut out as in Fig 3, adding 1 cm ($\frac{3}{8}$in) overlap along one edge of each piece.

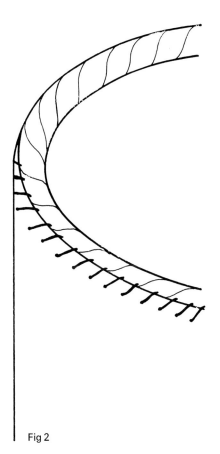

Fig 2

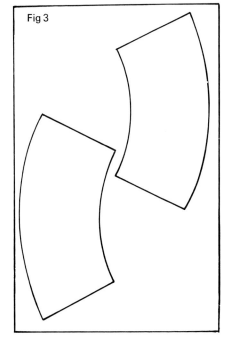

Fig 3

25

Lampshades

Pleated Paper Lampshade

This is a very good way of using up wallpaper left over after decorating to make a smart co-ordinating lampshade. You can make pleated lampshades almost any shape you like, they are made on two rings which can be the same diameter ; or the top one can be a little smaller, making the sides of the shade slope gently, or it can be much smaller making a real coolie shape.

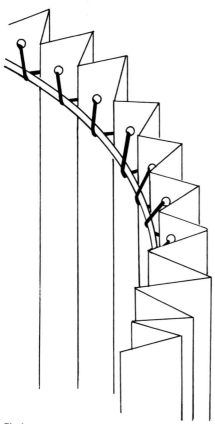

Fig 1

Whatever size upper ring you choose you will need double the circumference of the lower, larger ring for the length of the paper ; the width of the paper should be the height you want the lampshade. You will also need two lampshade rings, (one with light fitting), strong thread and either a leather punch or an office hole-punch.

It is not critical what size the pleats are, so long as they are at a right angle with the long edges and all the same size ; but about 2cm ($\frac{3}{4}$in) is an attractive size. It makes it easier if you can find a ruler, or cut a piece of card exactly this width. Rule pencil lines to mark pleats all along the wrong side of the paper. Crease the pleats, concertina fashion, along the ruled lines with finger and thumb.

Make a small hole in the centre of each pleat, about 2cm ($\frac{3}{4}$in) from each edge. Stick the short ends of the paper, overlapping each other, with clear adhesive, cutting off a pleat if necessary to keep the concertina effect in sequence. Take a length of double thread that matches the paper and insert it through the bottom holes, repeat with top holes, then draw threads up so that the pleated paper fits the rings. Knot the ends of the threads on the inside of the shade. Distribute the pleats evenly around the rings.

Take a long length of double thread and tie one end securely to the top ring ; take this thread into each section of the pleated paper and then around the ring, so that the paper is firmly lashed to the ring, as in Fig 1. Then tie ends of thread in a reef knot. Repeat with bottom ring. The pleats can then be adjusted evenly.

Lampshade Trimmings

There are many braids that can be bought and if a little care is taken a good match can usually be found. There is also a large variety of fringes, tassels and bobbles on the market for the base of shades. These braids and fringes can be stitched on to tailored fabric shades, but must be stuck on to stiffened fabric shades. Narrow velvet ribbon is better stuck on straight-sided shades.

One of the neatest trimmings for tailored shades is a crossway strip made of the same fabric as the body of the shade. This is a strip of fabric, cut on the bias (see page 10) about 2.5cm (1in) wide. The edges are folded in to the centre, like bias binding, and pressed, see Fig 2. This bias strip is then glued in place to cover the stitching. As the fabric on the strip is double, the adhesive should not show through to the front, if care is taken. As it is cut on the bias it has sufficient 'give' to be shaped around curves.

Side seams should always be covered first, the ends of these are then covered by the top and bottom strips. Where the ends of the strip meet, turn under 6mm ($\frac{1}{4}$in) at each end and stick with folded ends butted together as in Fig 3.

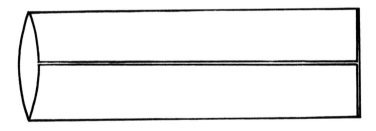

Fig 2

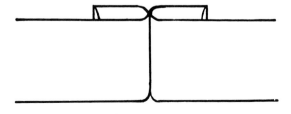

Fig 3

Table-linen

Choosing Fabrics

A fabric that can be laundered easily is the most suitable choice, as cloths and napkins will become soiled frequently. There are many very attractive dress cottons and cotton mixtures in exciting designs and colours on the market, the only problem with them being, that the narrow width makes one, or more, joins necessary. If these joins are well-planned and the pattern matched on the seams this problem is easily overcome. An ideal fabric is sheeting, which can be bought by the metre in plain colours and patterns, for it washes extremely well and is wide enough to make no seams necessary.

Calculating the amount of fabric
A cloth for a dining table should overhang the edge of the table by 30–35cm (12–14in).

For a square table measure the top surface of the table, then add overhang, plus 6cm ($2\frac{1}{4}$in) hem allowance on each side. If you cannot cut this measurement from one piece of fabric, arrange the seams as follows : let the complete width of fabric be the centre of the cloth, then cut a second length in half and join this to each side to make the overall size. In this way the seams will be at the sides and hardly noticeable.

For a round table use a measuring tape to measure from the centre of the table to the edge of the overhang (see Fig 1), then add 1cm ($\frac{3}{8}$in) hem allowance. Cut the fabric into a square twice this measurement ; if the fabric is not wide enough, make side joins

as for square cloth. Fold the square of fabric into four. Place the end of the tape-measure at the folded corner, see Fig 2, and mark a radius of this measurement from one edge to the other. Cut along the chalked line.

For an oval table measure the top of the table from centre to short edge, and from centre to long edge, then add overhang and 1cm ($\frac{3}{8}$in) hem allowance. Cut a rectangle this size (making side joins if necessary as before) then lay the rectangle of fabric over the table and hold it in place with some heavy books. Place the tape-measure on the edge of the table and mark the overhang—plus hem allowance—all round the fabric with tailors' chalk. Then remove fabric and cut out along chalked line.

For an oblong table cut as for square, but altering the table-top measurements to fit the table.

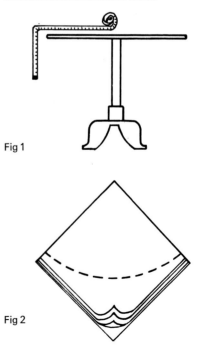

Fig 1

Fig 2

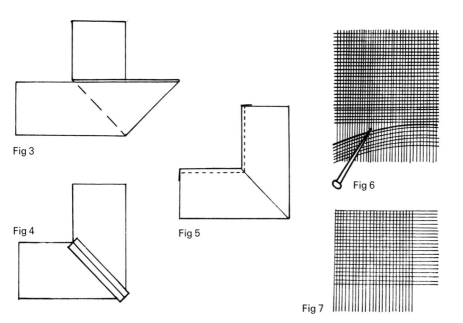

Fig 3

Fig 4

Fig 5

Fig 6

Fig 7

Hems and Edgings

For a square or oblong cloth a large hem allowance is given as a deep machined hem, with mitred corners, makes a very neat finish to a tablecloth. Tack the mitred corners in place, together with the rest of the hem, before machining.

To make mitred corners
Fold over 6cm (2½in) allowance at each corner and tack edges together along diagonal, Fig 3. Cut off surplus, leaving 6mm (¼in) turning. Machine seam and press flat, Fig 4. Turn hem over to wrong side, unpick a little of the mitre seam to allow 1cm (⅜in) of raw edge to be turned to inside, tack hem and corners, press then machine close to edge (Fig 5).

On round or oval cloths, make a narrow machined hem or bind the edges with bias binding.

Napkins

These should be about 40cm (16in) square ; when making round or oval cloths they can be made from the corner off-cuts. If you are making them to match square or oblong cloths, make mitred hems, but make hems about 2cm (¾in) wide. The machining of the hem can be done in contrasting satin stitch to add interest. Make the binding match for round cloths with a bound edge.

If linen or other coarse weave fabric is being used, the edge of the napkin can be given a pretty 'fringe' effect.

To make fringed edge
Make sure the edge of the napkin is cut quite true to the grain of the fabric. With a pin, pull away two or three strands along the cut edge, see Fig 6. Continue till an attractive fringe is formed, Fig 7.

29

Bed-linen

The materials for making one's own bed-linen are now widely available in stores and by mail order. At one time sheeting came in very few colours and almost no patterns, whereas nowadays the home furnisher wishing to make her own sheets, pillowcases, duvet covers, or the duvet (or continental quilt) itself is quite spoilt for choice.

A large saving is achieved by making a down, or feather and down mixture, filled duvet using the contents of an old eiderdown as the filling. If you are not sure of the quality of the filling, a sample can be sent to Aeonics Ltd (see List of Suppliers, page 64) who will test it for you. They also sell down-proof cambric and ready-made channelled casings if you do not wish to make your own.

If you make a duvet with synthetic fibre filling the saving is not usually very great, so it is worth shopping around and making careful costings before you start. The same applies when making bed-linen: having decided what design or colour you wish your duvet cover, fitted sheet, valance and pillowcases to be, compare the cost of the fabric with the ready-made articles; in most cases I think you will be pleasantly surprised.

Duvet

To avoid having cold toes in the night a duvet should be at least 46cm (18in) wider than the bed by at least the length of the bed, which allows an overhang about the size of a pillow at the end. The casing for the filling is made with channels so that the filling doesn't all slip into the corners. The casing must be made from down-proof cambric for a down-filled duvet; a washable synthetic fabric can be used for a synthetic-filled duvet.

To estimate fabric

You will need two pieces of fabric the size of the bed, plus 46cm (18in) overhang at the sides, plus 4cm (1½in) turnings length and width. You will also need five strips, each 5cm (2in) wide and each 4cm (1½in) shorter than the fabric length for a single bed; seven strips for a double bed. These strips can be joined if necessary.

To make

Lay rectangles of fabric on the floor, wrong side up (the shiny side is the wrong side of down-proof cambric) and draw lines running the length of the fabric, as in Fig 1. Draw five lines for a single bed and seven lines for a double bed; the lines should be equally spaced and the same on each piece of fabric.

Pin a strip along each chalked line on one of the pieces of fabric, then machine in place 1cm (⅜in) from the edge of the strip. Machine two sides of the fabric, right sides together, as in Fig 2. Fold the pieces of fabric over, and pin the other side of top strip to the top chalk line, then machine in place, 1cm (⅜in) from the edge of the strip, making the turning face the same way. Repeat with second and following strips, Fig 3.

Turn in 1cm (⅜in) on base and remaining side seam and topstitch to close. When stitching base seam, fold the end of the channel walls across their centres, making all the folds in the same direction, so that the topstitching closes the end of each channel. Make a second row of topstitching all around three sides of the case, leaving the top open for filling.

To fill the duvet
If you are filling your duvet with synthetic fibre you will need between $2\frac{1}{2}$–$3\frac{1}{2}$lb for a single size and $3\frac{1}{2}$–$4\frac{1}{2}$lb for a double size, depending on the size of your bed.

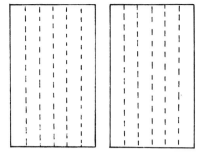
Fig 1

If you are using down or a down and feather mixture, you will need between 2–$3\frac{1}{2}$lb for a single bed and between 3–$4\frac{1}{2}$lb for a double bed, depending on the proportion of down to feather. The supplier will be able to give you exact amounts required.

If you are filling with down or feather, take the precaution before you start of wearing an overall, covering your head with a scarf and wearing a scarf as a face mask as the feathers fly everywhere. Choose an uncarpeted area to fill the quilt that is draught-free and easy to vacuum. A washing line rigged up over the bath or in the garage is often the best solution. Hang the casing with the openings at the top and fix to a clothes-line with pegs at one edge. Place a handful of filling in each channel, close channel with a peg and shake the casing gently so that the filling is pushed down. Continue distributing filling into channels, a handful at a time. When filled, turn inside 1cm ($\frac{3}{8}$in) of the open end of the casing and pin edges together, make two rows of topstitching to close.

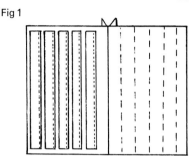
Fig 2

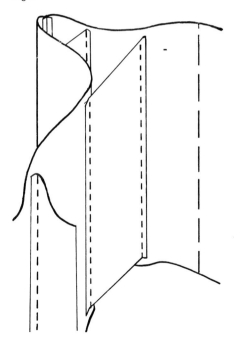
Fig 3

Bed-linen

Duvet-cover

To estimate fabric
The duvet cover is really just a detachable bag which should be made a little larger than the duvet, about 2cm ($\frac{3}{4}$in) on each side. Measure your duvet and add this allowance, plus 1.5cm ($\frac{5}{8}$in) turnings on each edge. You will need two pieces of fabric this size. A long, lightweight zip is the neatest fastening ; if you cannot get one long enough, about 80cm (30in), buy two zips slightly longer than half this size, and insert them so that they open from the centre, see Fig 1. Drip-dry polyester/cotton sheeting 228cm (90in) wide is sold in a very large selection of plain colours and patterns and is ideal, as it is wide enough to require no centre seam.

To make
Place the two pieces of fabric, right sides together, and pin and machine one side seam taking 1.5cm ($\frac{5}{8}$in) turnings and leaving a space centred in the seam large enough to insert the zip or zips. Oversew raw edges of seam and gap, press seam open and pin zip right side up to wrong side of opening, as in Fig. 2. Machine zip or zips in place, 1cm ($\frac{3}{8}$in) from zip teeth on right side of cover. Open zip and turn cover to wrong side. Machine other three sides and oversew raw edges. Turn cover to right side and press.

Fig 1

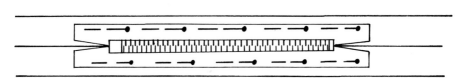

Fig 2

32

Fitted Bottom Sheet

With the advent of the duvet it was very important to have a tailored bottom sheet, which fitted around the mattress and would stay neatly in place. The corners of a fitted sheet are mitred but to make it easier to place around the mattress, elastic is threaded into the hem on each corner.

To estimate fabric

You will need a piece of fabric the size of your mattress, plus twice the depth of your mattress in each direction, plus another 10cm (4in) in each direction for hems and tuckaway.

To make

At each corner on the right side of the fabric, mark with tailors' chalk a line the depth of the mattress plus 10cm (4in) from each edge, as in Fig 3. Pin these two lines together to form a diagonal fold, as in Fig 4, and stitch along chalked line. Cut off fabric leaving 0.5cm ($\frac{3}{16}$in) turning next to stitching (Fig 5). Turn fabric to wrong side and stitch again, 1cm ($\frac{3}{8}$in) from edge to form french seam, as in Fig 6. Make a 1cm ($\frac{3}{8}$in) machined hem all round edge of sheet, leaving a small opening about 25cm (10in) from each corner. Insert elastic into each corner and gather corners lightly. Stitch ends of elastic to secure and stitch up openings.

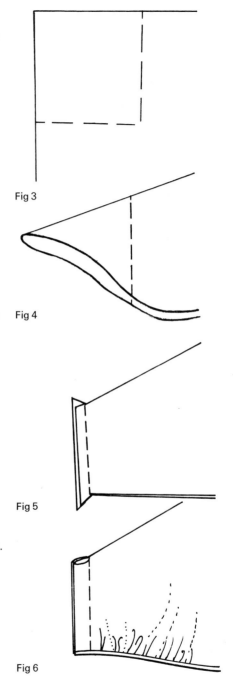

Fig 3

Fig 4

Fig 5

Fig 6

33

Bed-linen

Valance

The advent of the duvet, and easy bed-making, also meant the demise of the bedspread and the exposure of an unsightly strip of divan bed between the duvet and the floor. To fill this gap the old-fashioned valance has become popular once again. Ready-made valances come in two basic styles: an elasticated frill which clings to the edge of the bed-base, and a piece of fabric the area of the bed with a frilled or pleated border. I personally think that the second style is well worth the extra fabric, and the extra effort of placing it under the mattress, and instructions for making this type are given here.

Platform Valance with Frill

To estimate fabric

The piece of fabric the area of the bed which makes the platform need not match the border as it will not be seen; it can therefore be made from any inexpensive washable fabric, such as calico, and can be seamed to make up a rectangle the size of the bed (if you use calico wash it first, as it shrinks).

You will also need fabric to match or co-ordinate with your duvet cover for the frill. Measure the distance from the top of the bed-base to the floor and add 4cm (1½in) for turnings and hem; measure two long sides and the end of the bed—you will need twice this measurement for a generous frill. Buy sufficient fabric to make a strip this size, joined where necessary.

To make

Join the lengths of fabric to make up the frill with french seams (see pages 3, 21) then make a 1cm (⅜in) deep machined hem on one long edge, on the two short edges of the frill, and on one short edge of the platform piece of fabric. Run a gathering thread along the unhemmed edge of the frill. Pin the gathered edge of the frill to the three unhemmed edges of the platform, right sides together and adjusting the gathers evenly. Place pinned valance on bed-base and check that hem is level with the floor and that the seam between frill and platform will come just under the mattress. Adjust to fit, then machine. Oversew raw edges press and place under mattress.

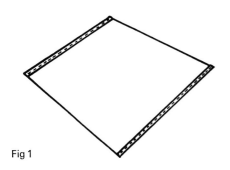

Fig 1

Pillowcases

This is a quick way to make four pillowcases with housewife style opening, which is a flap at the opening end that tucks around the pillow. To make four pillowcases 50 × 75cm (19 × 30in) :

You will need 170cm of 228 cm wide (67in of 90in wide) sheeting. Make 1cm ($\frac{3}{8}$in) machined hems along the two short sides of the piece of fabric, as in Fig 1. Then cut the fabric into four equal strips as in Fig 2. With right sides together, fold over 75cm (30in), then fold extending fabric over again, as in Fig 3. Machine along each edge taking 1.5cm ($\frac{5}{8}$in) turnings. Oversew seams and turn to right side.

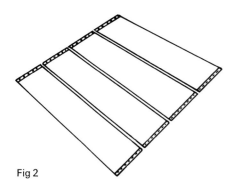

Fig 2

Fig 3

Loose Covers

A loose cover is a cover for an armchair or sofa that can be removed to be dry-cleaned or washed; the term 'loose' is misleading, however, as it should not look loose or baggy but should fit the chair or sofa snugly and should look as much like an upholstered cover as possible.

Choice of Fabric

Don't try to economise when buying fabric, as a well-made loose cover should last for years, as long as suitable fabric is used. The fabric must be strong enough to withstand the strain of wear and not shrink when washed or dry-cleaned.

Good fabrics for loose covers are linen union, repp and heavy duty needlecord. Always consult the dealer when buying fabric as to its suitability for loose covers. It is always a good idea to buy extra fabric so that any miscalculations will be catered for, and so that the places which get the most wear on the chair or sofa, such as the ends of the arm, can be fitted with arm guards which match the cover and are unobtrusive. Keep any left over scraps of material for repairs.

Calculating fabric
All chairs are different so it is much better to take measurements from your own chair rather than buy to a set rule; but keep in mind that an average two-seater sofa will take about 13m (14yd) of plain fabric and an average armchair will need 7m (7½yd) of plain fabric when you are shopping around for fabric. Of course if you are making the cover from patterned fabric you

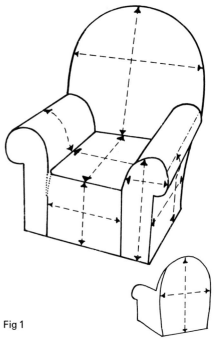

Fig 1

must allow extra for the repeat of the pattern; if the pattern is large buy at least two extra pattern repeats. You will also need about 1m (1yd) of fabric to cut into crossway strips to pipe the cover.

Figure 1 shows the measurements you should take of your chair and sofa; on each piece take the maximum measurement in each direction and add 4cm (1½in) in each direction for seams. You must also add 15cm (6in) for a tuck-in: a surplus fold shown by dotted line that is pushed down the sides of the seat to allow for the springing of the seat. Make a list of the maximum measurements of each piece including turnings and tuck-ins, remembering that you need two inside arms, two outside arms and two arm facings; then take a sheet of paper and draw on it an oblong representing the

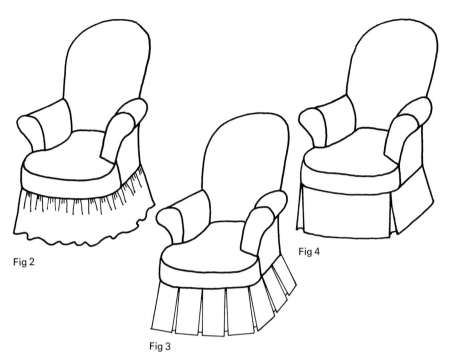

Fig 2

Fig 3

Fig 4

width of the fabric you propose to buy. Draw in each piece of fabric required until you have fitted them all in, (with the pattern running correctly, if you are using patterned fabric) then total up the amount required, adding an extra 1 m (1 yd) to your cutting plan for piping, and 1 m (1 yd) extra each for pattern repeats and for arm guards ; remember also to allow 4cm (1½in) seam allowance on all pieces and tuck-in on pieces that require it. If the chair has loose cushions, take measurements as for box cushion (page 9) and add this to the plan.

Frilled or pleated base
If you want a frilled or pleated edge at the base of the cover, measure the circumference of the chair at the point where the frill should start. For a *gathered frill* (see Fig 2) you will need a strip measuring 1½–2 times the circumference by the depth you wish the frill to be, plus 7cm (2½in) turnings for hem and seam. The strip can be joined where necessary but remember to allow for joins.

For *pleats* (Fig 3) you will need three times the circumference plus depth and turnings as above.

For *inverted corner pleats* (Fig 4) you will need the circumference plus the four pleats, 20cm (8in) each pleat, plus depth and turnings as above. See Fig 5 for different bases.

Tie-under base
If you wish the cover to tuck around the legs of the chair so that they show, allow 18cm (7in) at the base pieces all round the chair. A cord will run in a channel and tie the ends neatly under the chair.

Loose Covers

Cutting the Cover

For a really professional finish it is better not to attempt to make paper patterns, or use an old cover as a pattern, but to cut the cover on the chair. To ensure that the cover is symmetrical it is best to cut the main pieces out of folded fabric, on one side of the chair only.

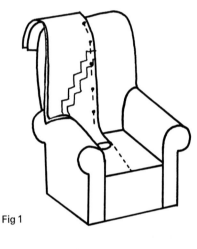

Fig 1

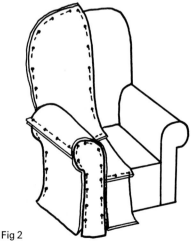

Fig 2

To prepare the chair for cutting, use a tape measure and tailors' chalk to mark a line down the centre of the chair, front and back. Cut the centre back (see Fig 1) first.

To do this, fold the fabric over lengthways, right sides together, and pin the fold down the line marking the centre back. When you pin the fabric, make sure you have allowed sufficient for a seam allowance at the top of the back, and make sure that if the fabric is patterned the pattern is placed centrally on the back, see Fig 1.

Cut the fabric allowing for tuck-in at back of seat and making the shaping around the arms generous as this can be trimmed when the cover is fitted. Cut piece for seat, cutting it double in the same way and allowing for turnings, tuck-in and considering position of pattern. Cut border piece and outside back in the same way. The arms, inside and out ,and the scroll pieces should be cut singly. You can use the fabric plan to cut these pieces out singly, as an oblong only, then pinning them to the double pieces and cutting out, as in Fig 2. When they have been cut out singly they can be unpinned and laid on fabric right sides together with the pattern matched, so that a second identical piece can be cut.

Remove the pins, unfold the folded pieces, then re-pin the entire cover, wrong side out on the chair. Place the pins close together and pin so cover fits smoothly, make any tucks necessary for a smooth fit at this stage. Don't attempt to fit the frill at this stage. Cut all turnings to 4cm ($1\frac{1}{2}$in) and cut notches in turnings so that pieces can be matched when unpinned for piping. See Fig 3.

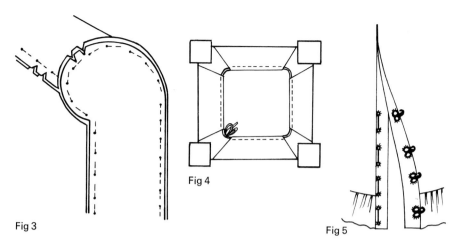

Fig 4

Fig 3

Fig 5

Unpin one back side seam for a chair, or two back side seams for a sofa and remove cover with pins in place. Unpin sufficiently to tack piping in place. Prepare piping as for cushions, (page 10). Nick edge of piping around scrolls. Machine seams, including piping and nicking turnings around curves. Oversew turnings. Leave back side seam, or seams, open for fastenings.

Finishings

For frilled edge replace cover on chair, wrong side out and pin gathered frill or pleats in place. Remove cover and machine, and make machined hem.

For tie-under finish place cover on chair and cut around legs. Use bias-strip to bind cut edge. Make 2cm ($\frac{3}{4}$in) hem along straight edges and thread with cord to draw up as in Fig 4.

Fastenings

Hooks and eyes sewn by hand to a facing on the piped side of the opening and a strap on the un-piped side is the neatest and most reliable form of closure. Cut a strip of straight fabric 6cm ($2\frac{1}{4}$in) wide and 1.5cm ($\frac{5}{8}$in) longer than each opening. Turn raw edges of strip under 1.5cm ($\frac{5}{8}$in) and machine to edges of opening. Stitch hooks and bars in place at 5cm (2in) intervals (Fig 5).

Loose Cushions

Make loose covers as for box cushions, page 9.

Loose Covers for Sofas

Make as for armchair but with openings on both back seams. When joining fabric for back and outside back pieces, centre one width of fabric in middle of back and join lengths either side, matching design as in Fig 1, before cutting rest of cover.

Arm Guards

Make up end of arm section as for cover, matching pattern to cover and piping scroll. Make machined hem around edge.

Squab Cushions

Squab literally means short and fat, but in soft furnishing terms it refers to a loose cushion that is shaped to fit either a dining chair or an armchair. On an upright, or dining chair, the squab cushion usually has ties by which it is tied to the back of the chair; in either case the cover for the cushion must follow its shape and contours exactly. I will give instructions for making a foam tie-on squab cushion for a dining chair, and a fitted cover for a squab cushion that fits into an armchair.

Squab Cushion for a Dining Chair

Make a paper pattern from the seat of the chair and have a piece of foam about 3cm ($1\frac{1}{4}$in) cut to this shape. As this thickness is not really enough to make a box cushion cover, which would probably look rather clumsy anyway, the edges of the foam must be rounded. To do this, apply Thixofix adhesive to the edge of the cushion, allow it to become tacky, then pinch the edge together, as in Fig 1. This will give the foam a rounded edge. Use the foam as a guide for cutting two pieces of fabric, larger than the foam all round to allow for the thickness of the foam and 1cm ($\frac{3}{8}$in) turnings. It is better to slipstitch the cover together after filling with foam, rather than inserting a zip as the zip would make the seam bulky.

Cut four strips of fabric about 3cm ($1\frac{1}{4}$in) wide and about 24cm ($9\frac{1}{2}$in) long for ties. Fold the ties in half lengthways with right sides together and machine the long edge and one short edge, taking 0.5cm ($\frac{1}{4}$in) turnings. Turn to right side by pushing through with a knitting needle and press.

On most seats it is necessary to make two darts or some gathers at the front corners. Make the darts or gathers in both the top and the base of the cover. Then pin the two sides of the cover, right sides together, including the ties in the seam; place the ties as in Fig 2, ensuring that they align with the back uprights of the chair. Machine front and back covers together, leaving sufficient opening centre back to allow the foam pad to be inserted. Turn cover to right side and press. Insert foam and slipstitch opening to close. Tie squab cushion to chair as in Fig 3.

Cover for a Shaped Armchair Cushion

A cover of this kind is basically a box cushion cover, but shaped to fit the contours of the cushion. A zip fastening is preferable in this cushion and should be inserted in the centre of the back gusset. As armchair cushions usually have a wider section in the front the zip must extend around to the sides about 7cm ($2\frac{3}{4}$in) to make it easier to insert the cushion pad.

Cut two pieces of fabric for the top and bottom of the cover, using the cushion pad as a guide for cutting; allow 1cm ($\frac{3}{8}$in) on all turnings. Cut a piece of fabric for the front gusset measuring from corner to corner by the depth of the foam plus turnings.

Cut the fabric for the back gusset the length of the zip, plus turnings; but make it 3cm ($1\frac{1}{4}$in) deeper than the depth of the foam plus turnings, to allow for the insertion of the zip.

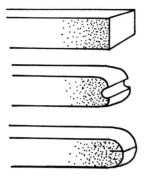

Fig 1

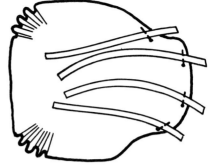

Fig 2

Fig 3

Cut the side gussets to fit between front and back gussets, as in Fig 4. You will also need sufficient No 2 piping cord to go around the top and bottom cover, and sufficient crossway strip to cover piping.

Apply piping to the top and bottom covers (see page 10 for piping techniques) clipping turnings. Insert zip in back gusset (see box cushion, page 9) and then join gusset pieces, pressing seams open. Leaving zip open, tack and machine gusset to front and back covers, right sides together and including piping in the seam. Turn to right side and press.

To insert cushion pad, roll back part of cushion cover as near to the front as possible. Tilt the foam to insert, then pull back cover.

Note: If your cushion is box sprung it will be too rigid to squeeze into the zip opening ; make cover in the same way but omitting zip, leave back and side gussets open at bottom edge to insert sprung cushion then slipstitch to close.

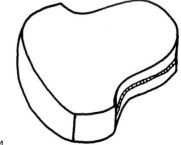

Fig 4

Upholstery

An upholstered chair or sofa has a cover that is permanently nailed in place and cannot be removed for cleaning. The traditional internal materials for upholstery are jute-webbing, springs, horsehair or coconut fibre; a chair properly upholstered with these materials should last for years. Pirelli webbing, which contains rubber, and foam are their modern counterparts for upholstery, and have made many jobs a lot easier.

When restoring a Victorian chair, I think the best results are achieved by using traditional methods; whereas the seat of a simple dining room chair or a buttoned head-board can be quickly made using foam. For this reason I will describe both the traditional and the more modern upholstery methods on the following pages.

Choosing a Top Cover

As the cover cannot be removed and is expected to last for many years it is very important that it should be strong and not soil too quickly. Dralon velvet, which is made of synthetic fibres, fulfils both these criteria as it is very hardwearing and is resistant to spills, which can be sponged off. It comes in a very wide range of plain colours and modern and traditional patterns. See list of suppliers on page 64.

Traditional Upholstery
Tools required

The specialized tools required for upholstery, modern or traditional, are few and not very costly; the expense involved in acquiring them will be recouped on the first job undertaken at home.

Figure 1 shows the basic tools as follows: 1 mallet with 10cm (4in) head; 2 ripping chisel; 3 cabriole or upholsterer's hammer; 4 webbing strainer; 5 spring needle; 6 small semi-circular needle; 7 bayonet needle; 8 regulator; 9 skewers (nos 1–7 are essential, 8 and 9 optional).

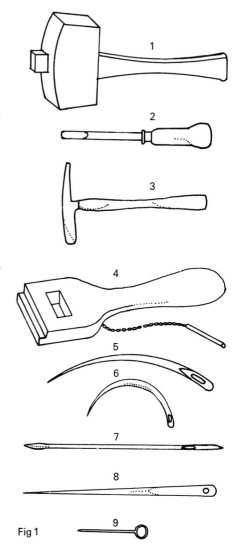

Fig 1

Materials Required

The materials required to upholster a button-back chair are : Jute webbing ; 10cm (4 in) eight gauge springs, scrim, coconut fibre, sisal laid cord, twine, tacks 1cm ($\frac{3}{8}$in) and 1.5cm ($\frac{5}{8}$in) ; horsehair and wadding.

You may be able to re-use both the horsehair and the springs (as long as they are not crippled) after you have stripped down the frame of the chair.

Estimate fabric for top cover by measuring old cover and have buttons covered professionally.

Stripping down the Frame

Unless you buy the frame of the chair already stripped, the first thing you must do is remove the old cover and all the old tacks, using the mallet and the ripping chisel.

To do this, place the end of the chisel against the head of a tack and tap the wooden end of the chisel with the mallet until the tack is pushed out of the wood. It is much easier to work with the chair at table height. Strip the chair in the following order, always working in the direction of the grain of the wood : remove canvas under the chair, then turn the chair the right way up and pull off glued-on braid, then remove top cover, take out all the stuffing, then remove webbing. Note how many strips of webbing were on the chair and how many springs and keep the piece of fabric with buttoning on for reference. The insides of old chairs are very dusty, so if possible work in a garage or workshop.

Applying Webbing

With the chair placed upside down on a table take the end of the roll of webbing and using the larger tacks tack to the centre underside with three tacks in a triangle as in Fig 2. Turn webbing over and place three more tacks in a reverse triangle, Fig 3. Thread other end of webbing into stretcher and use to pull webbing taut to other side of frame. Tack with three tacks, then cut off, turn over and tack gain. Continue until base is interlaced with webbing.

Applying Springs

Turn chair right way up and place springs on webbing, approximately 5cm (2in) apart. Thread spring needle with twine and sew each spring to the webbing with three stitches in three places, as in Fig 4.

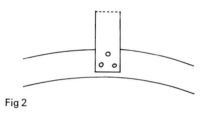

Fig 2

Fig 3

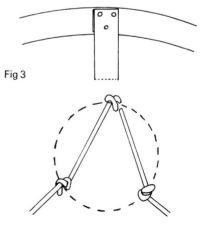

Fig 4

Upholstery

Lashing Springs

Tie one end of the laid cord around a large tack, and hammer to the side of the frame near a spring. Tie cord around two sides of the spring, as in Fig 1. Pull cord tight so that spring is held upright and lash in the same way to next and subsequent springs. Tie end of cord to tack on other side of frame. Repeat until all springs are lashed in both directions.

Take a piece of scrim large enough to cover the springs and tack over them to the side of the frame, turning edge of scrim over. Stitch tops of springs to scrim as in Fig 4, page 43. Make rows of large, loopy stitches all across the top of the scrim, about 20cm (8in) apart. Insert handfuls of coconut fibre into each loop until the whole seat is generously covered.

Take a piece of scrim large enough to go over fibre and down to the edge where the final cover is tacked. Turn edge of scrim over and place one tack in the centre of each side, pulling scrim firmly (see Fig 2). Tack scrim all round at about 5cm (2in) intervals, gathering scrim at corners.

Topstitching

The stuffing is now stitched into a firm edge which will give the seat its shape (see Fig 3).

Use the regulator to push stuffing into the roll being formed by the stitching so that it is really firm. Make loose looped stitches over top of scrim as before. Thread loops with horsehair that has been carefully unravelled with the fingers. Place a sheet of wadding over seat and cut off just above tacking line. Measure seat from edge to edge in both directions at widest points and cut a piece of top cover a little larger than this. With small tacks, tack in the middle of each side pulling fabric tight. Continue to tack from the centre of each side towards each leg, smoothing out any wrinkles.

Make small pleats above each leg. Tacks should be about 6mm ($\frac{1}{4}$in) apart. With a craft knife, cut off surplus fabric close to tacks. Stick gimp braid along edge of seat to hide tacks.

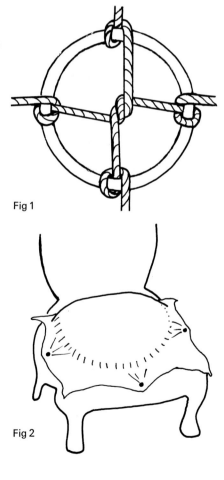

Fig 1

Fig 2

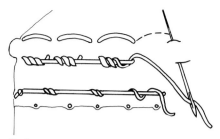

Fig 3

Back of Chair with Deep Buttoning

Apply webbing as for seat, but apply from the inside of the back. Tack scrim over webbing then tack a strip of scrim, about 10cm (4in) wide all around the outside edge of the back, filling it firmly with coconut fibre, and then stitching to scrim, as in Fig 4.

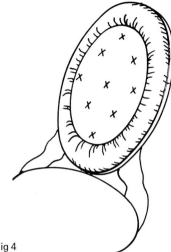

Fig 4

Edge-stitch this stuffed roll to make a firm edge for the buttons. Mark position of buttons on scrim as in Fig 4, or copying original position from fabric. Make looped stitches over button area and fill with well-carded horsehair. Mark same positions of buttons on wrong side of top cover, but making buttons one-fifth further apart in each direction. Make a well in the horsehair above each button position on back of chair, then cover the back with wadding.

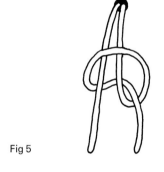

Fig 5

Thread bayonet needle with twine and push into a button position from the back, place button on thread then make a slip knot at back as in Fig 5. Thread on all buttons but do not pull the slip knots tight. Arrange pleats around buttons as in Fig 6 then pull knots tight. Tack fabric to edge, then cut off surplus close to tacks. Place layer of wadding on back then tack on piece of top cover, cutting off surplus close to tacks. Cover tacks with gimp.

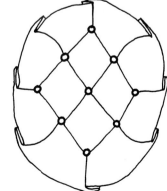

Fig 6

Upholstery

Upholstery Using Foam

Foam is now widely available, either already cut to standard sizes or cut to your own template ; and using foam and Pirelli webbing takes a lot of the hard work out of upholstery. Dunlop foam is available throughout the country but if you have any difficulty finding a stockist you can write to them and they will put you in touch with one. (See list of suppliers on page 64.) When buying foam always tell the supplier how you intend to use it, then he will be able to advise you about which grade to buy, as there are many different grades intended for different purposes.

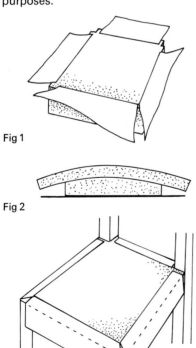

Fig 1

Fig 2

Fig 3

Re-upholstering a Dining Chair with Foam

These instructions are for a chair with a fixed or 'overstuffed' seat, for a chair with a loose or drop-in seat see page 47.

You will need Pirelli webbing ; hessian ; foam about 8cm (3in) thick of a grade recommended by the supplier ; large and small tacks as for traditional upholstery ; 12cm ($4\frac{1}{2}$in) wide calico strips ; Thixofix or other suitable adhesive ; top cover.

On most dining chairs the seat is curved or has insets at the back to fit around the back uprights. When all the old upholstery has been stripped off, in the same way as for traditional upholstery, make a paper pattern or template of the shape of the seat. Take the template to a supplier who will cut the foam to this shape for you, as it is quite difficult to cut foam neatly at home.

The Pirelli webbing should be interwoven in the same way as for traditional upholstery, but should be stretched by hand, without a webbing stretcher, and tacked with large tacks, without turning the edges over. To ensure that the edges of the foam seat have a firm profile, and to make an edge that can be tacked to the chair frame, the strips of calico should be stuck to the edges of the foam, cutting the strips to fit as in Fig 1.

If you wish your chair seat to have a domed effect, you can do this by padding the foam out from the underneath with another piece of foam, see Fig 2. This extra piece of foam should be about 2cm (1in) thick and cut 6cm ($2\frac{1}{2}$in) smaller all round than the seat, placed on the webbing with the seat foam on top.

When the calico strips are firmly stuck to the seat, pull them down and tack to the chair frame, Fig 3, leaving spaces in the calico to fit around the back uprights of the chair. The top cover will be tacked to the underside of the chair, measure over the seat of the chair, from left to right, and from front to back, and cut top cover a little larger all round. Place top cover on seat so that it will pull to the underside of the frame all round.

Using the large tacks, pull cover taut and place one tack in the centre of the front and one in the centre of the back, but without hammering the tacks all the way home. Tack cover in the same way in the centre of each side. Start to place permanent small tacks, about 2cm (1in) apart, working from the centre of each edge to within 1.5cm ($\frac{5}{8}$in) of the legs, pulling fabric taut as you tack. Tack into one thickness of fabric only, without turning under the edge of the fabric. Remove the four large temporary tacks. At the two back corners, cut a V shape where the cover goes back around the back uprights.

Turn in the raw edges of the V and tack cover down. At front corners, fold the cover as in Fig 4. The tacked edges of the cover, which show from the front, can either be covered with dome-headed tacks or gimp. Cut cover close to tacks on the underside of the chair. Cut a piece of hessian a little larger than the area of webbing on the underside of the chair. Turn under the raw edges of the hessian and tack in place on the underside of the chair to cover webbing.

Covering a Chair with Drop-in Seat

This type of chair can be covered in just the same way as an overstuffed chair, up to the point where the top cover is applied. The top cover should be tacked from the centre of each side, as for overstuffed seat. The seat should then be slashed at the corners as in Fig 5 ; then folded and tacked as in Fig 6.

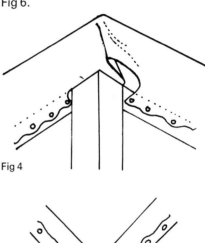

Fig 4

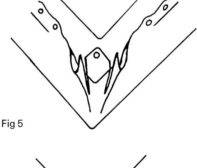

Fig 5

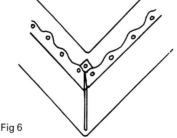

Fig 6

Upholstery

Buttoned Headboards

Using chipboard as the base and foam as the padding, a buttoned headboard can be easily made at a fraction of the cost of one bought in a shop. Dunlopreme D3 polyether foam, 6–8cm ($2\frac{1}{4}$–$3\frac{1}{4}$in) thick is ideal for this purpose. The base can be made of 1.5cm ($\frac{3}{4}$in) chipboard, either cutting the shape yourself with a fretsaw, or having it cut for you by a D.I.Y. store. Figure 1 shows some designs for headboards, with the position of the buttons marked, but you can also make a very attractive headboard from a rectangle.

Velvet is probably the most popular fabric for headboards and Dralon velvet is ideal. The diamond formation of the buttons looks most attractive if they are spaced further apart vertically than they are horizontally; for instance if the distance between the buttons from left to right is 14cm ($5\frac{1}{2}$in), the distance between them vertically should be 18cm (7in). The distance between buttons should never be less than 10cm (4in) or the headboard will look fussy and crowded.

As the top fabric, when pulled into the thickness of the foam at each button point, covers a larger area than that marked on the board, this extra fullness must be allowed for when marking button positions on the fabric. When buttoning into horsehair (see page 45) the button positions on the top cover are usually one-fifth further apart than those on the base.

When buttoning a foam headboard it is not usually necessary to allow this much extra fullness in the top cover. It is wisest to test the measurement, from one button position to another vertically and horizontally, before marking the top fabric. Do this after the button positions have been marked on the foam, by pushing the end of a tape-measure into one mark then measuring over the foam to the next and pressing the foam down again. Transfer these measurements to the wrong side of your top fabric.

In order to make the buttons push right down into the foam, a round hole should be cut in the foam at each button position. A good way of doing this is to sharpen the end of a length of round metal pipe with a file and use this to punch the holes in the foam. The pipe should be about 1.2cm ($\frac{1}{2}$in) diameter and after the hole has been punched the round piece of foam should be removed.

As the pile of the velvet should run downwards on a headboard, a large double headboard may be wider than the width of the fabric, making a join necessary. An upright seam running through the buttoning would look very ugly, so the join must follow the folds of the buttoning and be undetectable; this is called 'vandyking' and the vandyke join should be made before applying the fabric to the board as follows: mark button positions on the two pieces of fabric to be joined, then lay the two pieces of fabric so that they overlap each other by one row of buttons, as in Fig 2. Cut the fabric along the zig-zag lines allowing 1.5cm ($\frac{3}{4}$in) extra for turnings on each side. Pin and machine fabric along zig-zag join taking 1.5cm ($\frac{3}{4}$in) turnings. Do not press seam, but clip turnings at each button position, then turnings can turn in the direction of each fold when buttoning is 'set'.

To make

Make a paper template the shape you want the headboard to be, using one of the designs on this page or designing your own. Have chipboard and foam cut to size (foam can be joined by sticking pieces together with Thixofix adhesive). Mark button positions on foam and cut a hole at each position. Measure to estimate fabric needed for top cover, plus fabric to cover buttons. Have covered buttons made. Measure how much extra fullness is required on button positions on top cover, then mark positions on back of fabric,

making vandyke joins if they are required. Thread a bayonet needle with twine and working from the back, pass needle through top cover, through shank of button, back through top cover to back of board. Make a slip knot (see page 45) secured to a temporary tack at back of board. Set folds of pleats as in Fig 3, adjusting and tightening slip knot.

When pleats are set, the edge pleats should be tacked to the back, then tack all fabric round to the back of the board. Hammer home the temporary tacks to secure the slip knots. Cut off surplus fabric close to tacks at the back of work. A piece of felt can be glued to the back of the board to neaten.

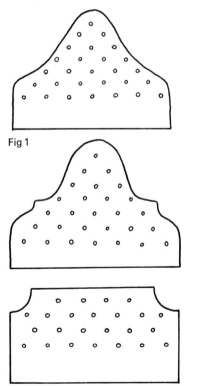

Fig 1

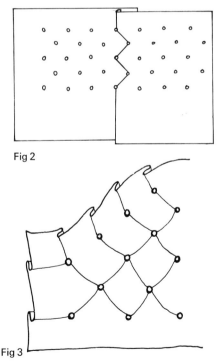

Fig 2

Fig 3

Curtains

Curtains are some of the most important items of furnishing in the home ; well-designed and well-made curtains can transform a room in the most dramatic way.

Before buying curtain fabric, you must decide what heading you want to use as it is the heading that determines the amount of fabric needed. You must also decide what length you want the curtains to be (see page 51).

The curtain track should be chosen and fixed in place before you can measure up the amount of fabric you will need. It is the width of the curtain track that must be measured, *not* the window, and the distance from the track to the floor or sill will determine the curtain length.

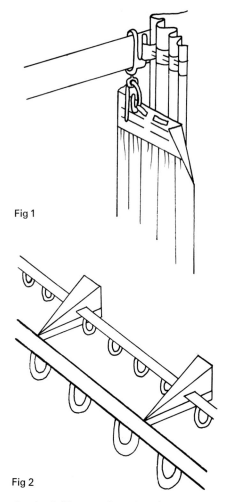

Fig 1

Fig 2

Curtain Track

The curtain track should always extend either side of the window so that the curtains can be drawn right back from the window where they will not obstruct any light.

Curtain tracks can be as plain or as fancy as you want them to be. There are plastic tracks that look like a neat white strip when the curtains are drawn back and are then, like most tracks, completely covered by the heading, when the curtains are closed. These tracks are easy to put up yourself and can be curved to go around bay windows. On many tracks of this sort, the curtain lining can be hung separately from the small rings below the hooks (Fig 1).

There are many tracks with patterns and different metallic finishes and fancy finials, and there are even tracks that look like curtain poles. Tracks can be supplied with a cording mechanism so that the curtains can be drawn back from each side with cords to avoid touching the curtains. This can usually only be done on a straight run and not on a bay. There are also double tracks, to enable nets and curtains to be hung from the same brackets ; the outside track takes the curtain and the slim track behind, the net, Fig 2.

When choosing a track, consult a

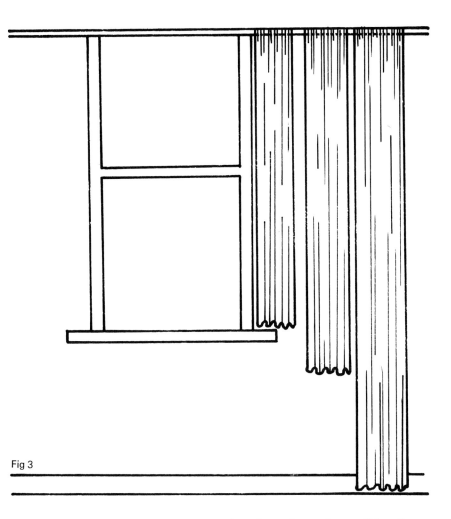

Fig 3

reputable dealer and make sure the track you have in mind is suitable for both your windows and the fabric you want to use ; for instance, some plastic tracks are not strong enough to support floor-length velvet curtains. Most tracks can be screwed either to the wall or to the ceiling, so decide which fixing you require.

The length of your curtains will depend on the style and shape of your windows, but there are three basic lengths to choose from : sill length, 1.25cm ($\frac{1}{2}$in) from the window sill ; between the sill and the floor, 15cm (6in) below the sill ; floor length, 1cm ($\frac{3}{8}$in) above the carpet pile or floor, see Fig 3. To this length add 20cm (8in) for top and bottom hems ; each width of fabric must be this length if you are using plain fabric ; if you choose patterned fabric you must allow one motif or pattern repeat per width after the first width.

Curtains

Headings

There are three main types of headings, plus variations on these themes. Each type of heading calls for a specific amount of fabric, and if the correct amount of fabric is used a very professional result can be achieved.

1 Basic gathered heading

1 *Basic gathered heading tape* comes only in a narrow finish, approximately 2.5cm (1in) wide, and it is usually the cheapest tape to buy. It is suitable for most types of fabrics although I think it looks best on sill length, or below-sill length, curtains in lightweight fabric, as it has a pretty, 'cottage window' effect. Using this heading tape is the cheapest way to make curtains, as it requires only $1\frac{1}{2}$ times the width of the curtain track.

2 *Pinch pleat heading tape* available in deep finish, approximately 9cm ($3\frac{1}{2}$in) and narrow finish, approximately 4cm ($1\frac{1}{2}$in). It is suitable for light or heavyweight fabrics and requires twice the width of the curtain track. A curtain fabric with a bold design is enhanced by a pinch pleat heading, as the plain area between the pleats shows off the design.

3 *Pencil pleat heading tape* also available in deep and narrow finish, this heading requires the most fabric, $2\frac{1}{2}$ times the width of the curtain track, but looks magnificent with velvet or other heavy plain fabrics.

52

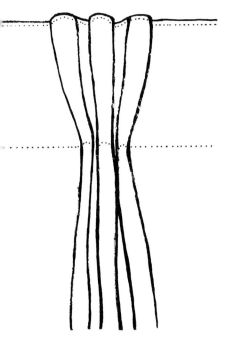

2 Pinch pleat heading

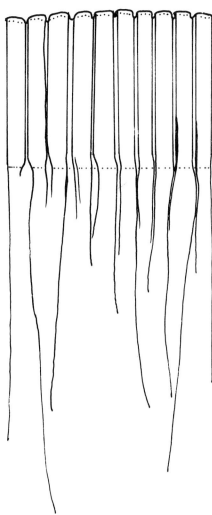

3 Pencil pleat heading

There are also heading tapes which give a 'smocked' effect and a heading tape which gives cylindrical 'cartridge' shaped pleats, each pleat can be padded out with a paper tissue to give rounded fullness. Many heading tapes come in both deep and narrow finish because obviously sill length curtains on a tiny window would look top heavy with a deep heading, whereas floor length curtains look rather skimped with a narrow heading. The price per metre of the heading tapes increases with the depth of the heading and the complexity of the pleating, and also varies according to the fibre composition of the tape. Lightweight headings have been specifically designed for use with sheer and net fabrics, and there are also heading tapes to which a detachable lining can be hooked.

Curtains

Unlined Curtains

Fix the track in position before you start to make the curtains, then choose a heading and calculate the fabric needed by measuring the track (including the overlap where the curtains meet) and the 'drop', the finished lengths of the curtains. Add to the track measurement the fullness required by heading tape, 4cm ($1\frac{1}{2}$in) for each side hem, and as the selvedges will be cut off to prevent the seams 'ruching', add 1.5cm ($\frac{5}{8}$in) at each edge of each width of fabric. The fabric can be cut into a half width to make up the fullness, always make the curtains too full rather than skimped. Add to the drop measurement 20cm (8in) for hem and headings and one pattern repeat per width, after the first width, for patterned fabrics.

Cutting Lengths

It is very important to cut the fabric on the true grain ; clear an area of floor so that the fabric can be laid out flat. Find the true grain by pulling out a thread at right angles to the selvedge and cut along this line. Measure and cut the first length of fabric, starting at the top of a pattern repeat if the fabric has a design. To cut subsequent lengths with the pattern matching, lay first length on top of fabric to be cut, as in Fig 1. Pin fabrics together then cut the next length.

Having cut required number of fabric lengths, cut off all the selvedges, as they will cause the seams to pucker. Pin and sew the lengths together, using a large machine stitch. The seams in unlined curtains must be finished so that raw edges will not show on the window side, use either a self-bound seam, Fig 2, or a machine-felled seam, Fig 3. Use a large machine stitch in both cases.

Self-bound seam
The advantage of this method is that no machining shows from the front of the curtain. Machine lengths, right sides together, taking 1.5cm ($\frac{5}{8}$in) turnings, trim one of the edges to within 3mm ($\frac{1}{8}$in) of the sewing line. Fold the wider turning over, turning 5mm ($\frac{1}{4}$in) of the raw edge under, and machining to the other turning, close to the first row of stitching, as in Fig 2.

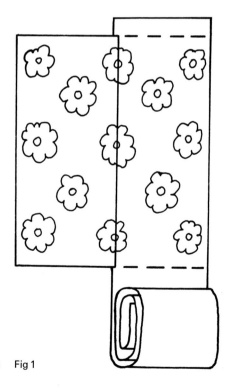

Fig 1

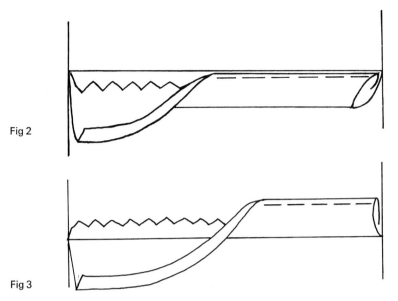

Fig 2

Fig 3

Machine-felled seam

Machine lengths and trim one turning as above. Turn longer turning under as above but machine to wrong side of fabric, as in Fig 3.

Side hems

Firstly turn under 1.5cm ($\frac{1}{2}$in) and press, now turn 2.5cm (1in) under and tack. Machine close to fold with a large machine stitch.

Stitching heading to top edge of curtain

Individual instructions come with most heading tapes but as a general rule a 1.5cm ($\frac{5}{8}$in) hem is pressed and tacked at the top edge. The heading tape is then tacked along its outer edges leaving 3mm ($\frac{1}{8}$in) between the top of the tape and the top of the curtain. At each end of the tape the cords must be pulled out, the surplus tape cut off and the edges of the tape turned under and

tacked so that the cords will pull freely.

Machine all round the outer edges of the tape, ensuring that the top and bottom rows are stitched in the same direction, and taking care not to stitch over the cords. The cords are then carefully pulled up to form the pleats. Do not cut off the surplus cord. When the curtains are washed or dry-cleaned the tape should be pulled out flat. A cord tidy can be bought on which the surplus cord is wound, the cord tidy then hooks into the back of the tape.

Hang the curtains from the rail and pin up the hem. Hang the curtains for about two weeks before machining the hem in case the curtains drop. Then machine a deep hem. Pull the curtains back, running your hands down the pleats so that they form neatly, then wind a couple of pairs of old tights around each curtain to 'set' the pleats. Leave in place for 24 hours.

Curtains

Lined Curtains

Cut required lengths of fabric, as for unlined curtains, and cut the same lengths of sateen lining. Cut off selvedges and machine curtain lengths together and the lining lengths together. Press all seams open. Turn over and press 4cm (1½in) down the side of each curtain. Lay the lining on the curtain, with wrong sides together ; the lining must now be 'locked' to the curtain. Locking is rows of loose, vertical stitches catching the lining to the curtain. Two or three rows of locking stitches should be made per width of fabric. Use sewing cotton that matches the curtain.

Make sure that lining and curtain are aligned with each other and smoothed out flat. Fold back the lining in the centre of the curtain and make locking stitches 10–12cm (4–5in) apart, as in Fig 1. Catch only two threads of

curtain in each lock stitch and end rows 23cm (9in) from lower edge of curtain.

When rows of locking stitches are complete, cut off excess lining along each outside edge of curtain, so that 2cm (¾in) of lining is turned under, leaving 2.5cm (1in) of right side of curtain showing at each side. Stitch heading to top of curtain and lining, as for unlined curtains.

Hang curtain from rail and pin up hem to correct level. Turn over 5cm (2in) of raw edge of hem to make deep double hem and press. Mark corner of hem with a pin, as in Fig 2. Unfold one turnover of hem and fold diagonally as in Fig 3. Fold corners up to make a mitred corner, Fig 4. Tack hem in place and re-hang curtains for two weeks, in case they drop, then adjust hem if necessary, and slipstitch mitre and curtain hem. Make a 2.5cm (1in) machined hem in lining, so that a 2.5cm (1in) margin of curtain hem shows below lining.

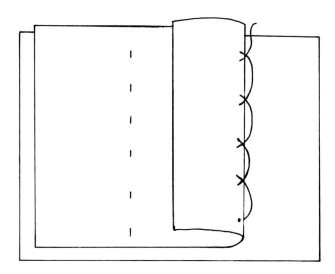

Fig 1

56

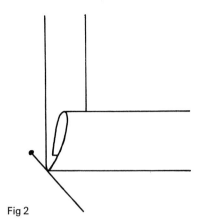

Fig 2

Headings for Curtain Poles

Curtain poles with chunky curtain rings are very popular and can be bought in wood shades, brass finish and a variety of bright colours. Both pencil pleat and pinch pleat heading tapes are available in 'underslung' versions ; that is one where the hooks are situated at the top of the tape where they are attached to the curtain pole rings. The curtains are made in exactly the same way, except that the drop measurement must be taken from below the pole.

Café Curtains

A very attractive way of using decorative curtain poles is to make café headings for your curtains. The café heading can either have a channel through which the curtain pole is threaded, making curtain rings unnecessary ; or curtain rings can be stitched to the top of each scallop.

An alternative café heading is a castellated edge, where the pole is threaded through the tabs ; café curtains traditionally consist of an upper and a lower curtain for each window, each with its own curtain pole, so that they can be drawn or opened independently of each other.

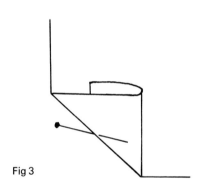

Fig 3

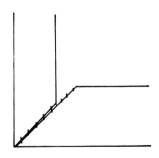

Fig 4

57

Curtains

Scalloped Café Heading

A To make a heading to be used with curtain rings

Fix the curtain poles in place at the window first, then all measurements can be taken from them. Measure the width of the pole, excluding the finials; the gathered skirt of the curtain should be $1\frac{1}{2}$ times this width, plus 6cm ($2\frac{1}{2}$in) for the side hems. The café heading should be the width of the pole, plus 3cm ($1\frac{1}{4}$in) turnings.

Measure the drop of the curtain from just below the curtain ring, and make the skirt of the curtain this deep (this allows for a deep hem). The depth of the heading strip should be 28cm (11in). If you are using lightweight fabric for the curtain you will also need mediumweight, iron-on interfacing half the depth of the heading strip.

Fold the heading strip fabric over lengthwise with right sides together, and work out your scallops from this fold allowing 1cm ($\frac{5}{8}$in) turnings at each end. Each scallop should measure 8–10cm ($3\frac{3}{4}$–4in) in circumference; and there must be a margin 3–4cm ($1\frac{1}{4}$–$1\frac{1}{2}$in) wide between each scallop. Use a compass to draw the scallops on to a piece of paper, with margins at each end and between each scallop. Add any surplus equally to the two end margins.

Cut out scallops and margins, adding 1cm ($\frac{3}{8}$in) turnings, machine, then nick turnings on curves, as in Fig 1. Gather up skirt of curtain and adjust gathers to fit heading. Tack to front of heading, right sides together, taking 1cm ($\frac{3}{8}$in)

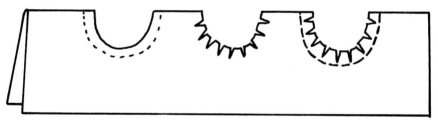

Fig 1

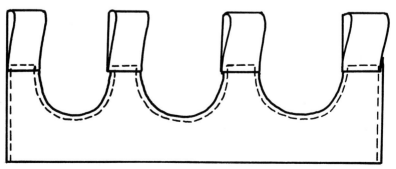

Fig 2

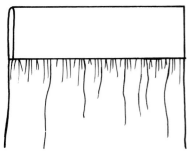

Fig 3

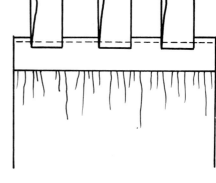

Fig 4

turnings. Machine in place. Turn heading to right side and press. Slipstitch the other side of the heading to skirt of curtain, close to stitching. Sew a curtain ring to the centre of each margin, or tab.

B To make a heading with a channel for curtain pole

Measure heading as for A, but add to the depth of the heading the measurement of the circumference of the curtain pole, plus 2cm (1½in). Make skirt depth and width the same as for A.

Fold heading fabric in half, as for A. Draw a line from this fold, the measurement of the circumference of the pole plus 2cm (¾in), and start scallops from this line. Continue margins up from line to fold. Cut out and stitch as for A. Attach skirt as for A. Turn to right side, push out margins with a pencil and press. Fold margins over to back of heading, check size with pole, and pin in place. Machine around curves and across base of margins to form loops, as in Fig 2. Slipstitch back of heading and make a deep machined

hem at the base of the curtain, making the curtain the required length. Remove one finial from pole, thread pole through looped heading then replace finial.

Castellated Heading

Measure skirt as for A. Gather skirt and bind with a 12cm (4¾in) wide strip, the length of the curtain pole plus turnings, see Fig 3. Cut strips of fabric 10cm (4in) wide ; making them as long as the circumference of the pole, plus 3cm (1¼in). Fold strips lengthwise, right sides together and stitch taking 1cm (⅜in) turnings. Turn these tubes to right side and press so that seam is centred on wrong side and 1cm (⅜in) is turned to the inside at each end of strip. Fold strips in half lengthwise so that turned in ends match.

Pin a folded strip at each end of bound curtain edge, then space strips equally about 8cm (3in) apart and pin 1.2cm (¼in) from bound edge, see Fig 4. Machine along bound edge of curtain, close to edge and 1cm (⅜in) from edge, including ends of strip in stitching.

Making Furniture

Having mastered the basic skills of home sewing it is very easy to create useful items of furniture for the home, using the knowledge you have and a little imagination. The following instructions show how to make a coffee table that converts into an overnight bed ; and how to transform a plain whitewood box into a padded window seat.

Coffee Table/Overnight Bed

(pictured on the cover)
You will need two slabs of polyether foam, Dunlopreme D17 is ideal. The slabs should be 18cm (7in) thick and 92cm (36in) square. Cut calico into strips 10cm (4in) wide and glue these to the foam slabs with Thixofix adhesive to make a hinge as follows : lay the two slabs flat, side by side with two 18cm (7in) edges touching. Stick a strip of calico along their central join, see Fig 1. When the adhesive has set, fold one slab on top of the other and stick another strip of calico so that it backs on to the first hinge, see Fig 2. Calico strips can also be stuck along all the edges of the slabs to prevent foam being chipped off.

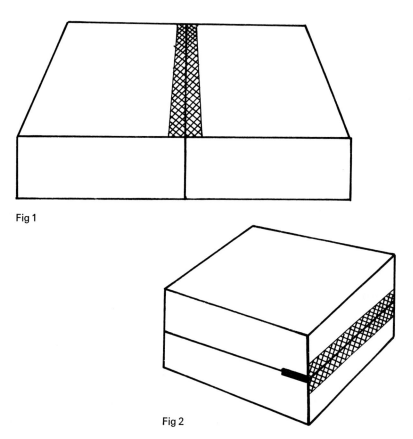

Fig 1

Fig 2

60

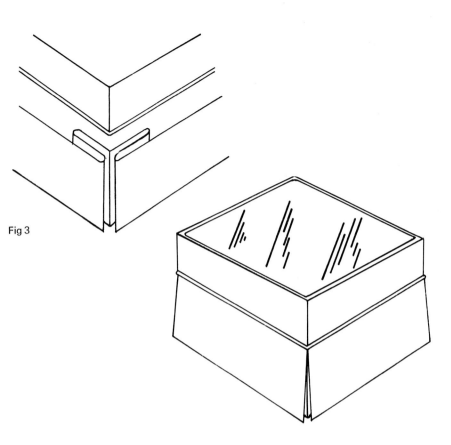

Fig 3

To make the cover

You will need 3m (3¼yd) of 122cm (48in) wide furnishing fabric : linen union or a cotton mixture that can be washed is most suitable. You will also need 0.5m (½yd) of contrasting plain fabric and 4m (4¼yd) of No 2 piping cord. Cut out a piece of fabric 94cm (37in) square and then cut four border pieces 94 × 14cm (37 × 5½in) ; for the skirt cut four pieces 104 × 30cm (41 × 12in). Take 1cm (⅜in) turnings throughout. Stitch border pieces to top fabric, as for the box cushion (page 9). Make up piping (see page 10) and stitch to edge of border. Stitch skirt pieces together, along short edges, and press the seams open. Make inverted pleats at corners, as in Fig 3, so that skirt fits borders. Tack and stitch skirt to border, including piping in the seam. Fit the cover on the foam and pin up a deep hem, so that the cover just touches the floor. Machine hem and press.

The covered foam can now be used just as it is ; or, if a piece of glass is cut to fit the top, as a coffee table. The cover can be removed and the foam unfolded to make a 92 × 184cm (3 × 6ft) overnight bed.

Making Furniture

Window Seat

Any strong wooden box of suitable size can be converted into a window seat—look in a junk shop for an old wooden school tuck box or something similar.

Have a piece of 8cm (3in) thick polyether foam cut to fit the top of your box. You will also need sufficient furnishing fabric to cover the top and sides of your box, inside and out, and sufficient 4oz terylene wadding to cover the sides of the box, inside and out; Copydex adhesive; a staple gun or hammer and small tacks; a curved needle; sufficient contrasting fabric to cover the inside of the box; Thixofix adhesive.

Making padded lid
Glue foam to lid of box with Thixofix adhesive. Make a box cover without a base to fit the foam-covered lid of the box, but make the sides of the cover extend 2.5cm (1in) beyond the edge of the lid so that they can be tacked or stapled to the inside of the lid of the box, as in Fig 1. Cut pieces of fabric to fit the outsides of the box, plus 1cm ($\frac{3}{8}$in) turnings at sides and sufficient turnings at the top and bottom of the box to turn over the edge of the box. Machine the sides of these pieces together, leaving one side open. Press seams open. Cut pieces of wadding to fit the outsides and insides of the box and glue in place with Copydex.

Place the machined side-pieces around the box, right side out, making the open side come at a back corner. Using the curved needle, ladder stitch this open side together so the cover fits

tightly around the box (see page 3). Turn the top edges of the cover over to the inside of the box and tack or staple in place. Turn the bottom edges over to the base of the box in the same way. Cut a piece of wadding and a piece of inside fabric slightly larger than the inside base of the box and staple or tack in place a little way up the sides. Cut and machine inside pieces of fabric in the same way as outside pieces. Turn over top and bottom edge and press so that they exactly fit inside of box. Slipstitch in place with curved needle. Cut a piece of inside fabric slightly larger than the inside of the lid. Turn under edges and press to fit exactly. Slipstitch in place. If required a strip of the side fabric can be stitched to make a hinge, to be tacked or stapled to the lid and the inside of the box as in Fig 2. To finish off the window seat a decorative fringe can be stuck around the base of the box using Copydex, see Fig 3; the box makes a useful seat and can also be used for storage.

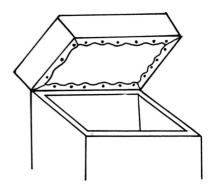

Fig 1

62

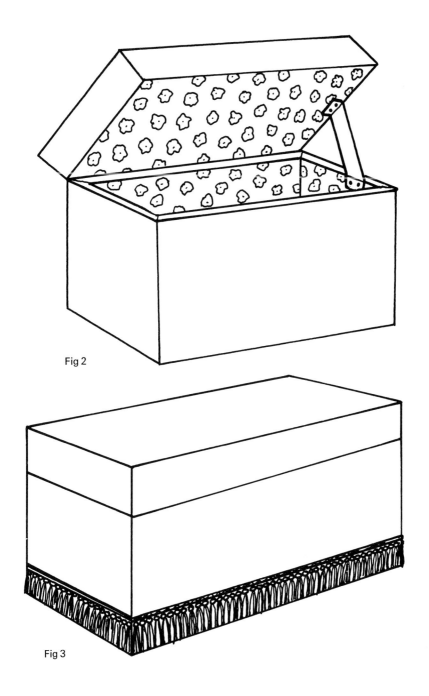

Fig 2

Fig 3

List of Suppliers

Polystyrene Granules
Arrowtip Plastics Ltd,
31/35 Stannary St, Kennington Rd,
London SE11
Send SAE for price list

Foam
Retail Sales Dept,
Dunlopillow, Pannal, Harrogate,
N. Yorkshire HG3 1JL
Information on local foam stockists

Thixofix Adhesive
Dunlop Semtex Ltd,
Chester Rd, Erdington, Birmingham
B35 7AL
Information on adhesives and stockists

**Duvet Casings, Down-proof
Cambric, Analysis of Down,
Sheeting**
Aeonics,
Block 8, 92 Church Rd, Mitcham
Send SAE for catalogue

**Furnishing Fabric of all kinds,
Sheeting, Terylene Wadding,
Lampshade Frames and Materials**
John Lewis,
Oxford St, London W1 (and branches)

**Heading Tapes, Curtain and other
Trimmings**
Rufflette Ltd,
Chester Rd, Manchester M15 4JD
Information on local stockists

Furnishing Trimmings of all kinds
Distinctive Trimmings & Co Ltd,
17 Church St, Kensington W8
and
11 Marylebone Lane,
London W1M 5FE

Upholstery Tools
Buck & Ryan Ltd,
101 Tottenham Ct Rd, London W1
Send SAE for price list

**Upholstery Materials: Webbing,
Wadding, Coconut Fibre, Twine
Laid Cord, Springs, Foam**
Turnross & Co,
130 Pinner Road,
Harrow, Middx
Personal shoppers only

Springs, Webbing, Foam
The House of Foam,
62–64 Hoe Street,
Walthamstow, London E17

British Library Cataloguing in Publication Data

Sullivan, Caroline
  Making soft furnishings. – (Penny pincher; 12).
  1. Drapery   2. Slip covers   3. Bedding
  4. Upholstery
  I. Title   II. Series
  646.2'12   TT387

  ISBN 0–7153–7752–3

Cover illustration: Fabric 'Celeste' by Margo International Fabrics Ltd, 11 Masons Arms Mews, London W1. Lamp base from a selection at British Home Stores. Foam by Dunlop.

Illustrated by the author

© Caroline Sullivan, 1979

First published 1979
Second impression 1984

Printed in Great Britain
by Redwood Burn Ltd, Trowbridge
for David & Charles (Publishers) Limited
Brunel House   Newton Abbot   Devon

Published in the United States of America
by David & Charles Inc
North Pomfret   Vermont 05053   USA